ANXIETY IS YOUR SUPERPOWER

DR WENDY SUZUKI

The information in this book is not intended to replace or conflict with the advice given to you by your GP or other health professional. All matters regarding your health, including your mental health, should be discussed with your GP. The author and publisher disclaim any liability directly or indirectly from the use of the material in this book by any person.

First published in Great Britain in 2021 by Yellow Kite
An Imprint of Hodder & Stoughton
An Hachette UK company

First published in the United States in 2021 as *Good Anxiety* by Atria Books,
An imprint of Simon & Schuster, Inc.

1

Interior design by Erika R. Genova

A CIP catalogue record for this title is available from the British Library

Trade Paperback ISBN 978 1 529 33537 8
eBook ISBN 978 1 529 33238 4

Printed and bound in Great Britain by Clays Ltd, Elcograf S.p.A.

Hodder & Stoughton policy is to use papers that are natural, renewable and recyclable products and made from wood grown in sustainable forests. The logging and manufacturing processes are expected to conform to the environmental regulations of the country of origin.

Yellow Kite
Hodder & Stoughton Ltd
Carmelite House
50 Victoria Embankment
London EC4Y 0DZ

DR WENDY SUZUKI

Medical Disclaimer

This publication contains the opinions and ideas of its author. It is intended to provide helpful and informative material on the subjects addressed in the publication. It is sold with the understanding that the author and publisher are not engaged in rendering medical, health, or any other kind of personal professional services in the book. The reader should consult his or her medical, health, or other competent professional before adopting any of the suggestions in this book or drawing inferences from it.

The author and publisher specifically disclaim all responsibility for any liability, loss, or risk, personal or otherwise, that is incurred as a consequence, directly or indirectly, of the use and application of any of the contents of this book.

Some names and identifying characteristics have been changed.

In loving memory of my father, Mikio Suzuki, and my brother, David Koshi Suzuki.

Thank you. I miss you. I love you.

CONTENTS

Anxiety is Your Superpower

INTRODUCTION

We live in an age of anxiety. Like an omnipresent, noxious odor we've grown used to, anxiety has become a constant condition, a fact of life on this planet. From global pandemics to crashing economies, to intense, daily family challenges, we all have plenty of justifiable reasons to feel anxious. The relentless twenty-four-hour news cycle and the constant stream of social media just add to this unease; we are surrounded by too much information to filter and too much stimulation to relax. The stress of daily living seems inescapable. Is feeling anxious inevitable?

Yes . . . but not in the way we usually think about it.

My early days of investigating and writing on this subject began in my lab as a neuroscientist at New York University. At the time, I never really thought of myself as an anxious person. That is, until I started to notice the words used by my subjects, friends, lab members, colleagues, and even myself to describe how we were all feeling:

"worried"
"on edge"
"stressed out"

"distracted"
"bored"
"pessimistic"
"unmotivated"
"nervous"
"ready to snap"
"defensive"
"frightened"
"unable to sleep"

Sound familiar?

A simple Google search shows that 18 percent of the American population—about 40 million people—suffer from one of several anxiety disorders, including panic disorder, PTSD, and generalized anxiety disorder (GAD). And yet, the numbers represented by these formal diagnoses are a mere scratch on the surface of anxiety's real population impact. Hundreds of millions more across the globe suffer from lower-grade, nonclinical yet persistently draining anxiety—the garden-variety type that pretty much all of us experience at one time or another. You know those worries that keep you awake at night even though you're exhausted? Or the continual to-do list that makes you feel like you are never able to fully take a break? Perhaps feeling so distracted that you can't sustain your attention long enough to read a full magazine article, never mind think through a problem? Have you ever experienced a sense of detachment that prevents you from connecting with family and friends the way you'd like to? You may be familiar with one or all of these signs of what I call "everyday anxiety." Yes, anxiety has many ways of showing up in our lives. And even if you don't *feel* anxious, you may still agree that modern living is almost always stressful.

Recent estimates suggest that anxiety shows up in our lives and affects a reported *90 percent* of the population—a truly astounding number of people, me included, who often resign themselves to the idea that we have no other option than to accept that anxiety—in whatever shape it takes—will be more or less a constant fixture in our lives, draining energy and causing unhappiness, negative body image, decreased sex drive, and difficulty truly connecting with our friends and loved ones. Perhaps we may go through good spells, where anxiety seems to disappear for a spate of time, but sooner than later, we end up feeling once again caught up in fears, worries, and an endless "what-if" list of concerns.

And because these symptoms are not considered severe or disabling, everyday anxiety often goes untreated—even though its side effects are enormously disruptive to our daily lives and relationships, our ability to get work done, our capacity to experience pleasure and enjoy ourselves, and our willingness to take on new, interesting projects, causes, or changes. Everyday anxiety can be a life-robber.

Too many of us accept these stressors as an unavoidable part of life. In fact, continual nervousness, sleeplessness, distraction, and dread seem like the appropriate response to the world we're living in. Indeed, some may not experience anxiety as something inside of them but think of it as part of the overall stress that exists outside them, as if it's a thundercloud they can get caught under if they don't run for cover fast enough.

When I first got interested in anxiety, I wanted to apply my groundbreaking research on movement and the brain (the subject of my first book) to help people manage anxiety more effectively. I aimed to address the anxiety crisis I saw all around me—around the NYU campus where I teach, in our high schools where I also do some of my research, among my talented and hardworking friends and colleagues, and what I had been observing throughout my travels around the world that reflected the statistics I was reading about. I believed, and my own research confirmed, that exercise, proper nutrition, and meditation could reduce and buffer against anxiety. But what I didn't appreciate at first was just how complex anxiety is; that if we simply approach it as something to *avoid*, *get rid of*, or *dampen*, we not only *don't* solve the problem but actually miss an opportunity to leverage the *generative power* of anxiety.

As I delved into the growing research, I discovered an altogether different side to anxiety. Sure, anxiety is unpleasant but it's *meant* to be. The more extreme examples of anxiety (still not the clinical level of severity, but the kinds that rise up at our most challenging and stressful moments in life) are downright destructive—no question about it. But what most people, including scientists, physicians, and therapists, often overlook is the fact that the anxiety we as humans feel is actually *essential* to our survival. In other words, anxiety is both bad *and* good for us.

This contradiction got my attention in a very personal way. When I was about to turn forty, I hit what I thought of as the proverbial wall of midlife. I felt incredibly dissatisfied with my life. I was twenty-five pounds over my normal weight. I worked all day, every day. I was frustrated, lonely, and feeling inadequate about my own ability to get myself out of the rut I was in. Always the scientist, I turned to what I knew best and decided to do an experiment on myself, which I eventually replicated using the gold standard—a randomized control study in my research lab. In the end, I discovered that exercise, nutrition, and meditation not only create measurable ways to lose weight and improve productivity, memory, and focus, but these mind-body interventions (the scientific word for "strategies") actually *change* the brain, and more specifically, change our relationship with anxiety.

Being able to measure these brain changes was a truly satisfying outcome of this research. But there was an additional silver lining that I experienced firsthand: After making changes to my lifestyle, I felt remarkably better. I was happier, more optimistic, and much less anxious. I must admit that I was at first only hoping to lose weight and get in better shape. I had not anticipated the intense uptick in my overall mental health and well-being. The changes I made were shifting how I was feeling, pointing me toward a new level of joy, engagement, and satisfaction that I never thought possible.

So, with anxiety on my mind, I returned to my earlier data to look more closely at what was behind the shift from negative emotions to positive. And as I synched up the data with the new cross-disciplinary analysis I was carrying out, I discovered that yes, my initial frustration and discomfort were actually neurobiological and psychological expressions of anxiety. At its core, anxiety can be explained as an arousal and activation of both brain and body when they encounter negative stimuli or stress. The brain and body are essentially interconnected. (Indeed, this interconnection is why I use the term "brain-body" to refer to the system as a whole.) When I began to trace the neurobiological roots of the relationship between anxiety and the more positive outlook, the boost in confidence, and the tangible increase in my happiness, I found that my arousal (i.e., anxiety) didn't suddenly disappear; rather it transformed from a negative state to one that was collectively more positive.

Yes, my anxiety seemed to be an inevitable part of a serious, competitive career. But I started to see anxiety as a kind of neuronal arousal or stimulation that had a range of different effects on my life. Like a form of energy, the arousal of anxiety takes on a positive or negative cast depending on how an individual responds to a particular stressor, or outside force. I realized that the positive feelings I was experiencing were actually neurobiological responses to the exercise, clean diet, and meditation I had sought out at the prompting of my negative thoughts, which had been prompted by negative responses to former stressors (too many deadlines, too many days without a break or prolonged rest, too many sugary, fatty dinners accompanied by little if any exercise). My anxiety had driven me to make the changes to my lifestyle that were now great sources of joy.

From this point of view, anxiety is not inherently bad. How we experience this arousal depends on how we (or our brain-body system) interpret and manage an encounter with an outside stressor. An outside stressor might trigger anxiety in the form of worry, sleeplessness, distraction, lack of motivation, fear, etc. But outside stressors can also elicit positive responses. For instance, some people become anxious before a public speaking event. For others, the idea of getting up in front of a crowd can be stimulating and exciting. One way of responding is not necessarily better than the other; it's more accurately a reflection of a person's way of managing stress at any given moment combined with their history. And if the response varies based on perception, then it is possible that we can actually take control of our responses.

....

This idea that anxiety is dynamic and changeable blew me away. Sure, anxiety is an inevitable feature of life, and none of us is immune. But understanding anxiety against this more fulsome backdrop has allowed me to stop struggling against it. Instead of treating my feelings as something I need to avoid, suppress, deny, or wrestle to the ground, I have learned how to *use anxiety to improve my life*. What a relief. Like all of us, I will always encounter bouts of anxiety. But now, I know what to do when those negative thoughts move into my mind like an unwanted roommate. I can recognize the signals and make adjustments that will take the edge off, calm my body, or settle my mind so I can once again think clearly and feel centered. What a boon to my life—personally, professionally, and certainly emotionally. I feel more satisfaction and meaning from my work. I have finally achieved a work-life balance, something that always seemed out of reach. I am also much better able to enjoy myself, find time for different kinds of pleasure, and feel relaxed enough to reflect on what matters most to me. And that's what I desire for you, too.

We tend to think about anxiety as negative because we associate it only with negative, uncomfortable feelings that leave us with the sense that we are out of control. But I can see another way of looking at it once we open ourselves to a more objective, accurate, and complete understanding of its underlying neurobiological processes. Yes, there are inherent challenges to taking ownership of patterns of responding that dictate our thoughts, feelings, and behaviors without our even realizing. If you tend to experience anxiety when you even think about speaking in public, your brain-body will more or less dictate that response—unless you consciously intervene and change it. But I saw evidence of the opposite: that we can intervene and create positive changes to the anxiety state itself.

This dynamic interaction between stress and anxiety made perfect sense to me because it brought me back to the primary area of my neuroscience research: neuroplasticity. Brain plasticity does not mean that the brain is made of plastic. Instead, it means that the brain can adapt in response to the environment (in either enhancing or detrimental ways). The foundation of my research into the improvement of cognition and mood is based on the fact that the brain is an enormously adaptive organ, which relies on stress to keep it alive. In other words, we need stress. Like a sailboat needs wind in order to move, the brain-body needs an outside force to urge it to grow, adapt, and *not* die. When there's too much wind, the boat can go dangerously fast, lose its balance, and sink. When a brain-body encounters too much stress, it begins to respond negatively. But when it does not have enough stress, it plateaus and begins to coast. Emotionally, this plateau might feel like boredom or disinterest; physically it can look like a stagnation of growth. When the brain-body has just enough stress, it functions optimally. When it has no stress, it simply lists, like a sailboat with no wind to direct it.

Just like every system in the body, this relationship to stress is all about the organism's drive for homeostasis. When we encounter too much stress, anxiety drives us to make adjustments that bring us back into balance or internal equilibrium. When we have just the right kind or amount of stress in our lives, we feel balanced—this is the quality of well-being we always seek. And it's also how anxiety works in the brain-body: It's a dynamic indication of where we are in relation to the presence or absence of stress in our lives.

When I started making changes to my lifestyle and began to meditate, eat healthy, and exercise regularly, my brain-body adjusted and adapted. The neural pathways associated with anxiety recalibrated and I felt awesome! Did my anxiety go away? No. But it showed up differently because I was responding to stress in more positive ways.

And that is exactly how anxiety can shift from something we try to avoid and get rid of to something that is both informative and beneficial. What I was learning how to do, backed up by my experiments and my deep understanding of neuroscience, was not just to engage in new and varied ways to shore up my mental health through exercise, sleep, food, and new mind-body practices but to take a step back from my anxiety and learn how to structure my life to accommodate and even honor those things at the heart of my anxious states. This is exactly how anxiety can be good for us. In my own research experiments at NYU, I have started to explore and identify those interventions (including movement, meditation, naps, social stimuli) that have the biggest impact on not only decreasing anxiety levels per se but also enhancing the emotional and cognitive states most affected by anxiety, including focus, attention, depression, and hostility.

And that realization of how anxiety works, my friends, became the subject—and the promise—of this book: understanding how anxiety works in the brain and body and then using that knowledge to feel better, think more clearly, be more productive, and perform more optimally. In the pages ahead, you will learn more about how you can use the neurobiological processes underlying anxiety, the worry, and general emotional discomfort to *lay down new neural pathways* and set down new ways of thinking, feeling, and behaving that can change your life.

Our inherent capacity for adaptation offers the power to change and direct our thoughts, feelings, behaviors, and interactions with ourselves and others. When you adopt strategies that harness the neural networks of anxiety, you open the door to activating your brain-body at an even deeper, more meaningful level. Instead of feeling at the mercy of anxiety, we can take charge of it concretely. Anxiety becomes a tool to supercharge our brains and bodies in ways that will resound in every dimension of our lives—emotionally, cognitively, and physically. This is the domain of what I call anxiety's superpowers. You will shift from living in a moderately functional way to functioning at a higher, more fulfilling level; from living an ordinary life to one that is extraordinary.

This book is about taking everything we know about plasticity to create a personalized strategy of adapting our responses to the stress in our lives and using anxiety as a warning signal and opportunity to redirect that energy for good. Everyone's particular flavor of positive brain plasticity will be a bit different because everyone manifests anxiety in unique ways, but when you learn how you respond, how you manage the discomfort, and how you typically cope and reach for that homeostatic balance, then you will find your own personal superpowers of anxiety. Anxiety can be good . . . or bad. It turns out that it's really up to you.

PART ONE

The Science of Anxiety

1

What Is Anxiety?

The daily stress of living can often feel like it's leaving us short of breath, literally and figuratively, as if getting through each day is like climbing a mountain. Our nights are often sleepless, and our days are marked by distraction and a difficulty shifting our focus away from bad things. We are filled to the brim with responsibility, worry, uncertainty, and doubt. We are overstimulated by everything from terror to FOMO (fear of missing out), regardless of whether this experience emanates from using Instagram, Twitter, or Facebook or reading news reports online. For a lot of us, anxiety seems like the only appropriate reaction to the state of the world.

People call it different things, but anxiety is the psychological and physical response to stress. The body does not know the difference between stress caused by real factors and stress generated from imagined or hypothetical situations. But by understanding the actual neurobiology of what triggers anxiety and what happens in our brains and bodies when it occurs, it's possible to learn how to parse our feelings into smaller pieces that can be moved around and managed. It also becomes possible to leverage the energy of anxiety for good. Anxiety really does work like a form of energy. Think of it as a chemical reaction to an event or situation: Without trustworthy resources, training, and timing, that chemical reaction can get out of hand—but it can also be controlled and used for valuable good.

· ANXIETY AS DETECTION OF THREAT ·

Imagine you are a woman in the Pleistocene epoch and part of a hunter-gatherer tribe. It's your job to forage near a shallow riverbed approximately five hundred yards from the nomadic tent encampment. Your twelve-month-old infant is strapped to your back as you reach down and search for edible shrubs alongside the river. Suddenly you hear a rustle nearby. You freeze immediately, stopping all of your movement. You crouch silently, so as to not disturb the baby and also to hide from a possible attacker. From this position, you listen for more rustling, trying to approximate the distance of the noise. Your heart begins to beat more quickly, adrenaline courses through your body, and you feel your breathing become jagged and shallow as you firm up your legs, ready to run . . . or defend yourself.

You are in the midst of a threat response: an automatic reaction to possible danger. If you stand up and catch sight of a large cat on the prowl, the anxiety response would no doubt be warranted and you'll either freeze, flee, or fight, depending on an adrenaline-enhanced evaluation of your best chances for survival. If you stand up and see that the noise came from a low-flying bird, your heart rate will slow down and return to normal. The adrenaline and feeling of fear will subside quickly. Your brain-body will reset to normal.

This is the first level of anxiety: an automatic processing of threat. This ancient part of our brain works so fast and automatically that we are barely conscious of its functioning. It's designed this way to ensure our survival. The brain sends signals to the body, which then reacts with increased heart rate, sweaty palms, a surge of adrenaline and cortisol, and a shutting down of the digestive and reproductive systems so that you can escape quickly or ramp up your strength to protect yourself and your offspring.

Now imagine another scenario, this time in 2020, where you live alone in a one-bedroom bungalow that backs onto an alley in a small suburban town. It's evening, and you are preparing a cup of tea to enjoy while watching a new episode of your favorite show. As you plug in your electric kettle and look for some cookies in the back of the cabinet, you hear a loud crashing noise coming from the direction of the back door. Your heart quickens and you freeze for a moment as you stare toward the door in fear: Is it an intruder? Are you about to be harmed? At first, you feel afraid to move, but then decide to peek out the kitchen window. As you do, you catch a glimpse of the neighborhood raccoon. Now that you think about it, just last week you had to pick up trash strewn across your driveway. You return to your tea and TV show but can't seem to settle down. You feel anxious and begin to wonder if your neighborhood is safe, if you should get a roommate, if you should move to another part of town or live in a high-rise so you don't have to feel so close to the street. Then you recall a story about a recent surge in break-ins and wonder if you should get a gun to protect yourself. You may find yourself feeling suddenly afraid and confused by the very thought of handling a gun. You turn off the TV, unable to enjoy your show, and decide to take an over-the-counter sleep medication to knock yourself out. You just want to sleep away all the terrible feelings.

These scenarios may be hypothetical and set millions of years apart, but they both embody the trigger and experience of anxiety, with different results.

First, let's take a look at what they have in common. Before you even become consciously aware of it, the brain detects the presence of a possible threat or danger and sends a signal to the body to ready itself to act. This response is in part physiological, as noted by the increased heart rate, the uptick of adrenaline, and the shallow breathing—these are all designed to prepare you to move quickly either to escape or defend yourself. The response is also emotional, triggered by the release of cortisol and noted by the immediate feeling of fear experienced in both versions. This threat response is often referred to as "fight, flight, or freeze," which happens in microseconds as your brain tries to figure out if a stimulus is indeed threatening and whether to flee as fast as possible, fight the potential threat, or freeze and act as though you're dead. This response is controlled by a specific part of our central nervous system called the sympathetic nervous system. With its main communication pathways located primarily just outside the spinal cord, this part of the nervous system works automatically and without our conscious control. It causes a cascade of reactions, including an acceleration of our heart rate, pupil dilation to better focus on the source of the threat, the queasy feeling in our stomach (an indication of blood rushing away from the digestive system to our muscles to enable fast action), and activation of our muscles to give us the power to either run or fight. The activation of all these systems is useful for dangerous situations. The physiological responses and the emotional experience of fear have to happen automatically in order to bring our attention to the threat of immediate danger.

In this way, anxiety is a hardwired threat response that our brain-body uses to protect us, as is the feeling of fear that reinforces the physiological changes.

In the first scenario, the woman's brain-body reset as soon as she determined she was not in immediate danger. In the second case, the woman's response continued even after she spotted the racoon. Her brain-body was caught up in the fearful feeling and she felt out of control. Professor Joseph LeDoux, a foremost neuroscientist and one of my NYU colleagues, explains that "fear states occur when a threat is present and imminent; states of anxiety result when a threat is possible but its occurrence is uncertain."[1] LeDoux is differentiating between fear (experienced in the presence of a real threat) and perceived or imagined danger (experienced emotionally as anxiety). The Pleistocene woman experienced a very sharp instance of fear along with her body's changes; the woman in the one-bedroom bungalow felt anxiety, a more prolonged, lingering emotional experience and one that she had trouble turning off.

Early research into anxiety focused on this preconscious, wired-in fear response as an evolutionary adaptive mechanism that is inherently natural and helpful. It's our brain's way of signaling us to pay attention to possible danger and is driven by our survival instincts. But as humans have advanced over time, and our world has become more complicated, structured, and socially driven, our brains have not completely caught up with the increasing social, intellectual, and emotional demands of our environment, which is why we feel anxiety as out of our control. This system, rooted in our more primal brain, is not adept at assessing the nuances of threats. Though the prefrontal cortex (i.e., the so-called top [executive] part of the brain critical for decision making) can help override these automatic fear-based responses through its intelligence, our primal brain, especially those areas related to these automatic threat responses, is still very much functioning as it was millions of years ago. This mechanism explains why the Pleistocene woman on the savannah and the contemporary woman in the town have, at first, very similar reactions to the noise. But it's only the more evolved woman who feels the lingering anxiety and the ensuing what-if list of worries. The Pleistocene woman goes on with her day once she has assessed that there is no reason to feel fear of imminent danger. The suburban woman is stuck in bad anxiety.

Scientists such as neuroscientist and primatologist Robert Sapolsky[2] have uncovered a challenging truth: Our brains have not changed *enough* in response to the vastly different, more complex social landscape in which we live. The first-level, automatic emotional responses to perceived threats are still generated and triggered deep in the more primal brain (often called the limbic system, which includes at its core the amygdala, insula, and ventral striatum), but our modern-day brains do not automatically discern between a real and an imagined threat; as a result, we often get stuck in anxiety mode.

Sapolsky has shown that this lack of discernment is why we individually and as a culture often find ourselves in chronic stress mode. We are unable to filter possible threats in our environment, and we are unable to turn off the emotional, mental, and physiological response to these threats even if they are imagined. These unregulated responses undermine our health and create what can become a near-constant negative feedback loop—the very essence of everyday anxiety.

Sapolsky and other researchers have shown that our brain-body systems are in a chronic activation of threat response—but not due to real dangers like lions on the savannah. Instead, our stress is exacerbated by living in loud cities; the stress of illness or poverty; the stress of emotional abuse or history of trauma. Big or small, seemingly inconsequential or traumatic, our brain-bodies do not automatically distinguish between potential threats and excessive stimulation—this causes the body to initiate the risk assessment protocol even when we can see that it was simply triggered by a passing fire truck. In truly disheartening research, Jack Shonkoff[3] and his researchers at Harvard's Center on the Developing Child have shown that early and continued exposure to extreme stress creates near-permanent maladaptations in the brain, affecting IQ and executive functioning. Such stressors include food insecurity and either direct or indirect exposure to physical or emotional abuse.

Indeed, our response to imagined threats is often the cause of the bad anxiety I'm talking about—the chronic worry, distraction, physical and emotional discomfort; the sense of doom and gloom, the second-guessing of the intentions of others; the feeling that you have no control over your life. It's all the "what-ifs" that come to us late at night when we can't fall asleep or are triggered by a health scare or some unexpected traumatic event in our lives. When we get stuck in that loop, we get caught in a brain-body response that becomes essentially maladaptive.

· SIMPLIFIED FEAR/STRESS/ANXIETY CIRCUITS OF THE BRAIN ·

Although scientists are still working to fully reveal all the brain areas and interconnected circuits involved in this threat or, more accurately, stress response, they generally agree that the brain areas shown in the following diagram are intimately involved. Threatening stimuli are quickly detected by the amygdala, a small almond-shaped structure deep in the temporal lobe. Think of the amygdala as the director of the primal brain, and the prefrontal cortex (PFC) as the director of the top or executive brain. When the amygdala responds automatically to threatening stimuli (real or imagined), it activates a wide range of areas, including the hypothalamus, which controls the sympathetic nervous system, to respond to the threatening or anxiety-provoking stimuli. The sympathetic nervous system, working through the brain's hypothalamus and pituitary gland, then activates the release of cortisol (a hormone produced in the adrenal glands), increases heart rate and respiration, releases glucose (energy), and prepares the body for action. (The sympathetic nervous system refers to the part of the autonomic nervous system that prepares the body for action in a fight-or-flight situation that is controlled by the hypothalamus.) In the modern-day stress response, this cycle happens, but the cortisol keeps being produced and released—this is the state of bad anxiety.

BRAIN-BODY FEAR AND EMOTION CIRCUTS

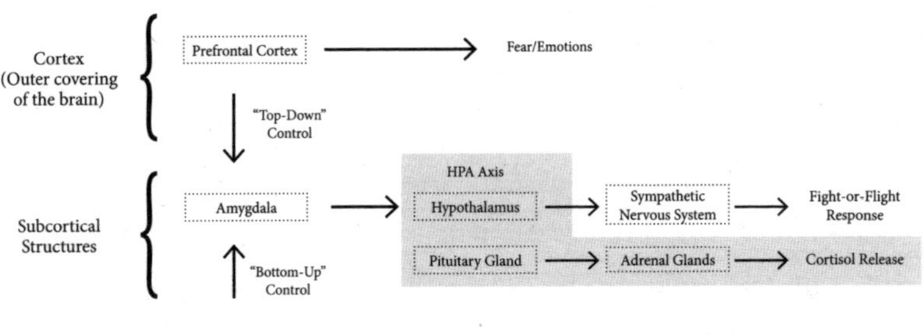

Fear/Threat/Anxiety-Inducing Stimuli
(i.e., Lion, rat, tax forms, job interview)

Figure 1: **Definitions**

Subcortical structures refer to any brain area below the cortex or outer covering of the brain.

"Bottom-up" brain processing refers to the automatic emotion-inducing signals from the lower brain to the cortex that assist in the processing of intense emotional reactions.

"Top-down" brain mechanisms typically arise from the prefrontal cortex and regulate the lower brain areas like the amygdala where intense emotional responses to stimuli are generated.

Sympathetic nervous system refers to the part of the autonomic nervous system that prepares the body for action in a "fight-or-flight" situation and is controlled by the hypothalamus.

HPA (hypothalamic-pituitary-adrenal) Axis refers to the complex interaction between the hypothalamus and the pituitary gland that, together, control the release of the stress hormone cortisol from the adrenal glands.

Another way to think about how the brain processes both emotion and thoughts is in terms of "lower-brain" or "bottom-up" functioning and "top-down" functioning. "Bottom-up" brain processing refers to the automatic emotion-inducing signals from the lower brain (i.e., the amygdala and other aspects of the limbic system) to the cortex to assist in the processing of intense emotional reactions. (The so-called lower brain also refers to any brain area below the cortex, i.e., "subcortical.")

"Top-down" brain mechanisms typically arise from the prefrontal cortex and regulate the lower brain areas like the amygdala, where intense emotional responses to stimuli are generated. It's the HPA (hypothalamic-pituitary-adrenal) axis that then manages the complex interaction between the hypothalamus and the pituitary gland, which together, control the release of the stress hormone cortisol from the adrenal glands.

· EVERYDAY ANXIETY VERSUS CLINICAL DISORDERS ·

It's helpful to think of anxiety as existing on a continuum, with clinical disorders on one end and everyday anxiety representing most of the spectrum.

In this book we are talking about everyday anxiety, but it bears mentioning that the number of people who have been diagnosed with clinical anxiety disorders is startling. Currently, 28 percent of the US population have been diagnosed with some form of anxiety-related disorder during their lifetimes—and that number is more than 90 million.

Psychologists and psychiatrists break down anxiety disorders into six general categories according to how symptoms develop and manifest:

Generalized Anxiety Disorder (GAD) is the most common group of symptoms that suggest a person has become overwhelmed with worry about any number of aspects of their life, including family and relationships, health, the state of their job or career, and money. People with GAD have trouble turning off their worries and often lose perspective about the reality of threat. According to the Anxiety and Depression Association of America (ADAA),[4] symptoms for GAD include:

- a persistent feeling of dread or impending danger
- rapid breathing
- trouble sleeping
- difficulty focusing or sustaining attention
- persistent gastrointestinal upset

Another common anxiety disorder is Social Anxiety Disorder (SAD), which is often referred to as social phobia. People experience fear of social situations, worries about how they are being perceived by others, and whether or not they belong or are accepted by a social group. In extreme cases SAD can trigger a panic attack (see below for more on panic disorder). According to the ADAA, many people with social anxiety disorder show strong physical symptoms, including:

- rapid heart rate
- nausea
- sweating

Some people with extreme anxiety develop a panic disorder, which is marked by sudden and intense experiences of alarm or fear. Per the ADAA, panic attacks are often accompanied by:

- sweating
- trembling or shaking
- sensations of shortness of breath or smothering
- feelings of choking
- chest pain or discomfort
- nausea or abdominal distress
- feeling dizzy, unsteady, light-headed, or faint
- chills or heat sensations
- paresthesia (numbness or tingling sensations)
- derealization (feelings of unreality) or depersonalization (being detached from oneself)

Obsessive-Compulsive Disorder (OCD) is a form of anxiety that shows up as compulsive behaviors or repeated thought patterns. At first, certain behaviors might be used as coping strategies to deflect the anxiety, but then the behaviors themselves become problematic and exacerbate instead of mitigate anxiety. According to the ADAA, people with OCD may be overly concerned about contamination and obsessed with cleanliness and a need for symmetry. Common compulsions include checking, washing/cleaning, and arranging.

Posttraumatic Stress Disorder (PTSD) is an all-too-common mental health condition suffered by many who have either "experienced or witnessed a natural disaster, serious accident, terrorist incident, sudden death of a loved one, war, violent personal assault such as rape, or other life-threatening events." Per the ADAA, about 8 million people (or 7–8 percent of the population) in the United States are living with PTSD. The disorder is characterized by three main types of symptoms:

- reexperiencing the trauma through intrusive distressing recollections of the event, flashbacks, and nightmares
- emotional numbness and avoidance of places, people, and activities that are reminders of the trauma
- increased arousal such as difficulty sleeping, problems with concentrating and focusing, feeling jumpy, and being easily irritated and angered

In addition to those listed above, some forms of anxiety disorders show up as specific phobias, where the anxiety is related to an object or irrational fear of something. Common phobias include fear of flying, fear of bugs, fear of enclosed places such as elevators, fear of bridges, and fear of heights. Phobias are so intense that people go out of their way to avoid the source of the fear and as a result curtail what they do on a daily basis.

It's important to keep in mind that all these types of disorders exist on a continuum and vary in intensity and duration in response to—you guessed it—the amount or type of stress. Many of these severe clinical disorders are managed by psychopharmacological medicines, which act to suppress or redirect the nervous system and dampen anxiety.

Let's take a look at the chart developed by the Anxiety and

Depression Association of America below. (LeDoux also includes this chart in his book *Anxiety*.)

WHICH IS IT?

Table 1.

Everyday Anxiety	Anxiety Disorder
Worry about paying bills, landing a job, a romantic breakup, or other important life events	Constant and unsubstantiated worry that causes significant distress and interferes with daily life
Embarassment or self-consciousness in an uncomfortable or awkward social situation	Avoiding social situations for fear of being judged, embarrassed, or humiliated
A case of nerves or sweating before a big test, business presentation, stage performance, or other significant event	Seemingly out-of-the-blue panic attacks and the preoccupation with the fear of having another one
Realistic fear of a dangerous object, place, or situation	Irrational fear or avoidance of an object, place, or situation that poses little or no threat of danger
Anxiety, sadness, or difficulty sleeping immediately after a traumatic event	Recurring nightmares, flashbacks, or emotional numbing related to a traumatic event that occurred several months or years before

Credit: Little House Studio

Looking at the list of characteristics, many of the signs of everyday anxiety are familiar and may not seem so serious. The clinical disorders are more intense and disruptive. What's important to keep in mind is that the underlying biology of anxiety is generally the same; it's the expression of it that varies. Anxiety is changeable, adaptable like any other feature of our brain. The very good news is that we e have the power to control everyday anxiety We can consciously use and apply the principles of neuroplasticity and learn how to manage the stressors of our environment more effectively so that anxiety is not in charge of us, but that we become in charge of anxiety.

· UNDER THE HOOD ·

While anxiety can manifest in so many different ways for so many different circumstances, there are some common traits that are important to point out. Let's take a look at what's happening under the hood of our brain-body when we experience anxiety as something out of our control. When anxiety gets in our way, we experience it as uncomfortable. We feel on edge and overstimulated and perhaps even hypervigilant. Too much cortisol is streaming through our brain-body and we can't seem to control its effects. Dopamine and serotonin levels, the two main neurotransmitters that make us feel both grounded and in charge, are either low or not communicating with each other properly. As a result, we have difficulty staying on task, which might make us procrastinate or unable to finish projects. We begin to feel pessimistic and perhaps a little hopeless. This state of emotional imbalance upsets our sleep cycle, our eating habits, and our overall health. We might begin to take the edge off these disruptive thoughts and feelings by drinking more alcohol or taking drugs, or eating too much of foods that feel good in the moment but end up making us feel kind of sluggish or sick. The longer the anxiousness lasts, the less we want to hang out with friends. We begin to withdraw and self-isolate, which in turn makes us feel lonely. We are so caught up in our worries we forget to ask for help.

Okay, that's a pretty dire description of anxiety, and yet it may seem familiar to most people because the idea of learning to control our everyday anxiety is relatively new. However, when you are in charge of anxiety, you will feel decidedly different. Anxiety's arousal, triggered by the stress response, will alert you to something that's bothering you—a sudden change at home or work, for instance. You pay attention and think through what's at stake: What does this change mean for you? For your loved ones? Can you control the situation? By organizing your thoughts around what you can control, you draw upon serotonin, dopamine, and cortisol to keep you focused on next steps. This action keeps you emotionally regulated and goal-driven. You ask for feedback from people you trust. You monitor your progress. You accept whatever mistakes you made or other ways that you may have contributed to the change and learn from that information. You stay open to new ideas. You make sure to take care of yourself, eating well and exercising regularly, so that you can sleep and give your brain-body time to recharge at night. You decide to avoid alcohol because you understand that it acts like a depressant and it disrupts your normal sleep rhythms. Soon, as you see your path forward, you begin to feel more relaxed and at ease.

The initial anxiety began similarly in these two situations, but the arousal of that threat-defense system took two very different pathways.

In the pages ahead, you will learn more about how we can shift our stress response so that it doesn't cause a cascade of negative effects. You will learn how to quiet and relax your body and calm your mind; you will learn how to redirect thoughts and reappraise situations so that you can make decisions that work for you. You will learn how to monitor how you respond to stress and tolerate uncomfortable feelings.

2

Leveraging the Power of the Brain's Plasticity

For over twenty years, the center of my research in neuroscience has focused on how the brain can change in response to the stimuli (aka stressors) in its environment. We know that the brain has evolved to grow, shrink, and adapt; it has evolved to find ways to work more efficiently. Indeed, the brain is driven at the cellular level to learn how to navigate a winding road on a dark night; recognize a particular species of falcon; learn a new piece of music by heart; or even sculpt a new shape no one has seen before. These are all examples of brain plasticity in action.

Today, we have a detailed understanding of the physical/anatomical, cellular, and molecular mechanisms that the adult brain uses essentially every minute of every day to change, learn, and adapt to the environment. But it was not too long ago, back in the 1960s, to be specific, that the prevailing wisdom of the time was that the adult brain could *not* change—that all the growth and development of the nervous system happened during childhood and up to a degree during adolescence, but once you reached adulthood, no more change.

In the early 1960s pioneer neuroscientist Professor Marian Diamond[1] of UC Berkeley and her colleagues had different ideas. They believed that the adult mammalian brain was capable of profound change; they just needed a way to demonstrate it. They came up with a simple but elegant experiment to test their idea. They decided to put a group of adult rats into what I like to call the "Disney World" of rat cages, with lots of regularly changing toys, a large physical space, and lots of other rats for company. They called this an "enriched" environment. They compared the rats who lived in the enriched environment with an equivalent set of rats raised in a much smaller space, with no toys and just one or two other rats for company. This was called the "impoverished" environment. They let the adult rats live in their respective environments for several months and at the end of that period they examined their brain anatomy to see if they could see any difference. If the other scientists at the time were correct, they should not have been able to see any difference in the brains whatsoever because these were unchangeable adult mammalian brains. By contrast, if they were correct and the adult brain had the capacity to change, they might see differences in brain anatomy. What they discovered has changed our understanding of the brain: The brains of the rats that lived in the Disney World cages were quantifiably bigger and more developed in various areas, including visual cortex, motor cortex, and somatosensory cortex. This was the first demonstration that an adult brain had the capacity to change, which we now refer to as adult brain plasticity. Further, Diamond demonstrated that the contents and qualities of the environment determine the type of change.

Importantly, this plasticity goes both ways. The changes (a demonstration of the brain's inherent plasticity) shown in the

Disney World experiments were positive, reflected by increased brain sizes (with later studies showing increases in neurotransmitters, growth factor levels, as well as higher densities of blood vessels) in the rats raised in Disney World. However, other environments or experiences can cause negative changes in the adult brain. For instance, when your brain-body is deprived of a stimulating environment or exposed to one that is violent, you see clear shrinkage of certain brain areas (particularly the hippocampus and prefrontal cortex, which we will talk about more in Part Two) and decreases in neurotransmitter levels (dopamine and serotonin), which help regulate our emotions and attention. If children are raised in environments of neglect, their brains will show a decrease in synapse number (synapses are the connections between brain cells where communication takes place), making thinking (i.e., cognition) less efficient and less flexible, two qualities associated with intelligence.

That the brain has this tremendous capacity to learn, grow, and change has been demonstrated in thousands of experiments—dating from the classic studies of Diamond and her colleagues to today. And understanding how our brains are plastic, flexible, and designed to adapt is at the very heart of believing that we can learn to control anxiety and actually welcome it. Indeed, at the heart of this amazing capacity for positive brain plasticity is our ability to learn and change our behavior—including our behaviors around our relationship to anxiety.

The brain's plasticity is what enables us to learn how to calm down, reassess situations, reframe our thoughts and feelings, and make different, more positive decisions.

Consider this:

- anger could block our attention or ability to perform
    - OR it could fuel and motivate us; sharpen our attention; serve as a reminder of what is important (i.e., priorities);

- fear could crash our mood; trigger memories of past failures; rob our attention and focus; or undermine our performance (i.e., cause us to choke under pressure)
    - OR it could make us more careful about our decisions; deepen our reflection; create opportunities for changing direction;
- sadness could flatten out our mood; demotivate us; or inhibit our social connections
    - OR it could point us to what is important in our lives; help us reprioritize; motivate us to change our environment, circumstances, or behavior;
- worry could make us procrastinate; or get in the way of accomplishing our goals
    - OR it could help us fine-tune our plans; adjust our expectations of ourselves; become more realistic or goal-directed; and
- frustration could stymie our progress; hinder our performance; or steal our motivation
    - OR it could innervate us and challenge us to do more or better.

These comparisons may seem simplistic, and yet they point to powerful choices that produce tangible outcomes. In other words, we have choices.

....

Anxiety, as typically experienced, is marked by negative emotions. Remember the list? "On edge," "pessimistic," defensive," "stressed out," "frightened"—these are all emotional states that generally make us feel bad. But it turns out that we are not impotent in our response to these emotions. Further, these emotions are not all bad; in fact, they provide us with important information about our state of mind and body. The sources of our anxiety are great pointers toward what we value in life. Does it take effort to shift those negative emotions to their positive versions? Yes. But they are also indications of what is important or valuable to us. Perhaps that worry about money is a reminder of how much we value financial stability; or the concern about privacy is a reminder that we need sufficient alone time.

Our negative emotions, then, present us with an opportunity to interrupt self-defeating cycles of thoughts, emotions, and behavior patterns that undermine our own stress response. A first step in gaining this control over anxiety is understanding how our emotions work.

· THE POWER OF NEGATIVITY BIAS ·

Anxiety is in many ways a catchall phrase for bad feelings. As I explained earlier, anxiety is, at its core, a full brain-body state of activation—cells are signaling to one another, energy ramps up, your brain-body is ready to do something. It's alert, it's ready, it's raring to go. When stuck in bad anxiety, this activation can trigger a host of feelings: nervousness, fear, discomfort, pain—the negative emotions that pull down our moods, distract us, and make us withdraw and isolate ourselves.

On the other side of these negative emotions are the wonderful, uplifting positive emotions: joy, love, humor, excitement, curiosity, wonder, gratitude, serenity, inspiration—the list goes on and on. These positive feelings drive our connection to ourselves and others; they ward off illness and keep us healthy by strengthening our immune system; they reward enjoyment and pleasurable behaviors so that we will continue to seek them out. All of these features of positive emotions also occur more or less automatically. We don't, for instance, tell ourselves to feel joy and suddenly feel joyful. So even though we need the negative emotions to protect us from danger and threat, we also need the so-called affiliative or positive emotions. The joy, love, excitement, and curiosity are what make us seek attachment and relationships; curiosity motivates us to learn and grow and understand the world around us; and desire urges us to mate.

And just like anxiety, our primary emotions can be defined as brain-based signals that either alert us to something bad (i.e., negative) or good for us. These basic or core emotions are hard-wired into our lower brain (including the limbic system) in order to protect us from threats and motivate us to seek what we need—shelter, food, companionship. But emotions have evolved to be much more complicated, which is why dealing with our anxiety can be so tricky.

One of the many reasons that anxiety seems to take over our mood is because we tend to default to the negative, not the positive. Our brains give negative feelings more salience and remember these feelings more vividly and intensely. As a result, they are more strongly encoded in our brains. Why do we tend to remember the negative emotions more than the positive? Why do we think of positive feelings as more the exception than the rule? In a basic way, we can answer these questions by seeing how our brains are wired to defend, which makes them prone to look for problems, detect danger, and avoid pain. These survival instincts are deeply wired into how our nervous systems are structured.

But from a narrative perspective, most scientists, doctors, psychologists, and journalists writing about emotions reflexively place them in positive or negative categories—as if negative emotions should be avoided when possible, as if they are necessarily bad for us. In this way, there's an unconscious bias against negative emotions of any kind—anger, fear, worry, sadness, frustration, etc. And the bent of science, which is often initiated as a way to explain or prevent disease, has spent less time researching the promotion of positive emotional states.

An example of an obstacle in the way of letting our positive emotions shine is a well-studied phenomenon called negativity bias.[2] This refers to the natural bias our brain gives to negative feelings over positive ones. A growing number of studies show that negative information not only attracts our attention more quickly than similarly powerful positive information but that negative information also influences people's evaluations more than the equivalent amount of positive information. We have all seen this, and likely know people who fixate on the things that have gone wrong, regardless of how many things went well. Maybe you recognize this behavior in yourself as well—that's the negativity bias rearing its ugly head.

Biologically and reflectively, it is no fault of yours that you tend to skew to the negative more than the positive. But if we could learn to remove the sting from these feelings, we could give ourselves more room to be flexible about how we process these emotions. What if we adopted a new point of view? What if we shifted our default orientation away from these negative emotions and instead focused on the goals that we want to achieve? What if we approached negative emotions as a challenge instead of a drag? What if we positioned these feelings as information to be curious about rather than dangers to avoid?

At a neurobiological level, all these different emotions—including the ones typically associated with anxiety—have a purpose: to draw our attention to something that is important. (In Part Two you will dive into significant research that shows how to channel emotional energy that could otherwise tip into bad anxiety; it relates to the neurobiology of a positive mindset, productivity, optimal performance, creativity, and more.)

One of the most important advances in affective neuroscience (the area of neuroscience that examines our emotional experiences) is that we have many more than five or six basic emotions. In 1980, Robert Plutchik[3] created this wheel of emotions to show how certain emotions have varying degrees of intensity or flavors.

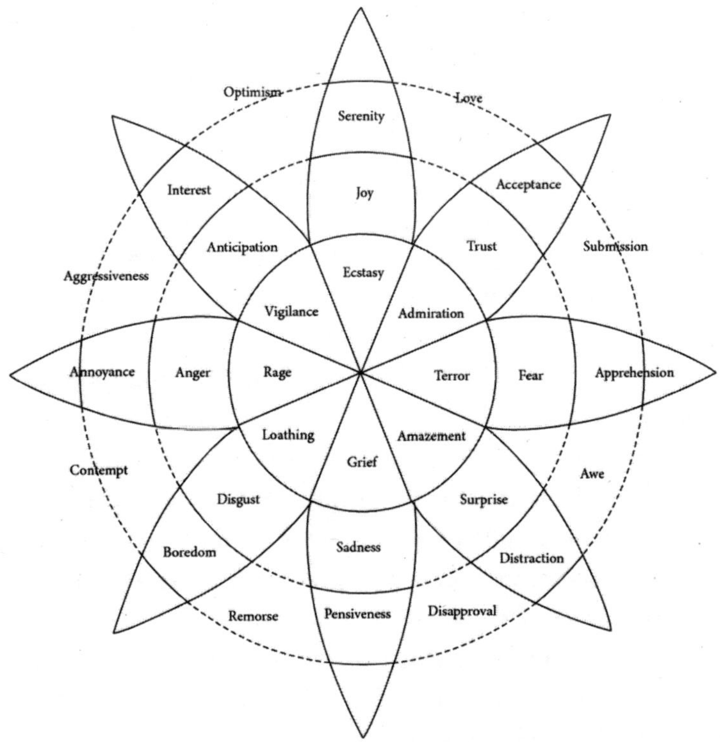

Figure 2. **Plutchik's Wheel of Emotions**

Looking at emotions from this point of view illustrates why it is so important to change the way we think about anxiety. Indeed, I suggest that anxiety can be a combination of negative and positive emotions and it therefore represents the entire wheel. As you move through the book, I hope you can become familiar with how both the negative and positive emotions of anxiety show up in your life—anxiety does not have to be a negative! Emotions always change!

· WE CAN REGULATE OUR EMOTIONS ·

The stress that causes anxiety is not going away, but we do have the capacity to "optimize" our response to it. Researchers including Alia

Crum, a Stanford University psychology professor, have shown how it's possible to use mindset and reappraisal techniques, both functions of the PFC, to approach stress as a challenge and an opportunity for "performance and growth".[4]

At the neurobiological level, what Crum and others are suggesting is part of a wider area of research and framing of the brain known as emotion regulation—the processes (both bottom-up and top-down) that help us manage all emotional responses, especially anxiety.

What do I mean by *regulate*? One expert on emotion regulation, James J. Gross, another psychology professor at Stanford University, defines emotion regulation as "the processes by which individuals influence which emotions they have, when they have them, and how they experience and express them."[5] Whereas historically scientists thought that emotion regulation was simply a top-down process controlling bottom-up emotions, now it's understood that there is a lot more bidirectional interaction between bottom-up brain areas (i.e., the limbic system) and top-down ones (PFC and other neural pathways it interacts with). Why? Because, as Gross says, emotion regulation is a complex system of "interconnected neural subsystems [that] monitor one another to varying degrees and are in continuous bidirectional excitatory or inhibitory interaction." He also points out that regulation is a set of processes that exist on a "continuum from conscious, effortful, and controlled regulation to unconscious, effortless, and automatic regulation."[6]

What does this mean in practice? The bottom line is this: Though anxiety might originate as some form of attention-getting signal to avoid danger, it doesn't necessarily have to cause discomfort, distraction, or otherwise interfere with our natural drive toward well-being and balance. We can learn to use awareness to reframe a situation, remove the perception of danger, and reappraise it instead as an opportunity to overcome a challenge and set down new learning (i.e., responses). We have multiple options for managing both the attention to the signal and the anxiety (the feelings), and if it gets to that point, the response itself. Our brain is a wondrous thing!

Our brain-body systems are in a constant drive toward homeostasis, that state of equilibrium between arousal and relaxation. Every system—from the nervous system to the digestive, respiratory, cardiac, immune, and others—is interacting and exchanging signals in order to respond to a stressor and then regain homeostasis. This is true of our emotional system as well. Our negative emotions arise to draw our attention to something that may be dangerous or present a risk, and then make some sort of change or adaptation to feel better. In other words, they have a positive purpose and are not meant to only have one volume. It is the same with anxiety: As a general form of negative emotion or discomfort, it's the brain-body's way of telling us to pay attention. Our built-in system for managing our negative emotions, of processing, responding to, and coping with negative emotions in particular so that we can maintain or return to homeostasis, is called emotion regulation.

Anxiety is a bundle of emotions that upset our ability to emotionally regulate. And they are meant to, because they are meant to draw our attention to an area where all is not as it should be. Once anxiety has triggered arousal, we are meant to apply our regulatory tools to those emotions in order to begin processing them; once we do so, anxiety should ebb and homeostasis should be restored. However, our ability to regulate our emotions is not always predictable. Indeed, the degree of one's capacity for emotion regulation varies depending on a number of factors—how we were raised, our lifestyle, and even our genetic profile. The good news is that we can learn to regulate our emotions more effectively. According to Gross's model of emotion regulation, we have five types of anxiety-management strategies that can help manage anxiety and other negative emotions. The five strategies identified by Gross include: situation selection, situation modification, attention deployment, cognitive change, and response modulation. The first four are strategies that can interrupt anxiety *before* it develops into an extreme state or a chronic one. The fifth is a regulatory technique *after* the anxiety (or other negative emotion) has occurred.

This model for understanding emotion regulation (referred to in the literature as the "modal model" defined by Gross) has been widely accepted and continued to be built on. Another neuroscientist in this field, Nils Kohn, adds to it by suggesting that we need to keep in mind that emotion regulation is both automatic (and therefore implicit and preconscious) and conscious (and therefore explicit and exerted through conscious awareness). Moreover, emotion regulation can be either functional and adaptive in nature (and therefore helpful to us) or maladaptive and dysfunctional.

Let's look at how emotion regulation plays out in real life. Say you are anticipating an important job interview after being let go from your former position six months prior. You are feeling pressure, self-doubt, and fear—fear of rejection, fear of failure, fear of not measuring up. The interview is four days away but you're already feeling nervous. When you even imagine walking through the door of the building, your hands start to sweat, your heart rate ticks up, and your breath becomes a tiny bit shallow. Next, you begin to imagine every possible thing that could go wrong: You might forget to bring your résumé, you might wear mismatching socks, or you might forget everything you know about why you're applying for the job in the first place.

One option is to avoid a situation that you expect will bother you or exacerbate your anxiety. Avoiding the situation (skipping the job interview) may alleviate the fear and stress in the near term; however, it clearly will not help you if, in the long run, you want or need the job in question. Gross calls this strategy situation selection.

Another option is to modify the current situation so that the anticipation or anxiety is made more tolerable or bearable. For instance, if you're experiencing anxiety about the pending interview, you could modify the situation by asking to do the interview over the phone or videoconference. This change to the situation enables you to exert some control over your anxiety and puts you more in charge of the feeling that it's bigger than you. Gross calls this situation modification. I call it a shift from bad to good anxiety. Your nervousness has not disappeared; it's simply under your control and being channeled.

A third option is referred to as attention deployment, which includes several ways you can avert your attention from the anxiety-provoking situation to something else that absorbs your attention. Parents use this technique frequently with their infants and toddlers. If the young child is afraid of dogs, for example, a parent could direct the child's focus to a funny face while the scary dog walks away. This is a kind of intentional distraction.

The fourth and probably most sophisticated of the strategies for emotion regulation is referred to as cognitive change. In this case, you actively and consciously reappraise or reframe your mindset or attitude: Instead of thinking about the job interview as a horrible way to spend your Friday morning, you reframe it as an opportunity to show yourself and your potential employer how much you know about the role and the company or organization; it also builds your confidence. You show up curious and excited to learn what he or she has to say. The reframe acts as a mental suggestion that reshapes the feeling of anxiety from one of dread and feeling overwhelmed to one of excitement and challenge.

Fifth, once you've managed to get yourself through the front door and seated in the interview, it's possible that the anxiety will rear its head despite the strategies you've used to mitigate it thus far. In this case, you are actively trying to suppress or mitigate the anxious feelings. Perhaps you do some breathwork (e.g., deep breathing, which is one of the fastest and most effective ways to calm the entire nervous system) or you drink some water. If it was not a job interview that got you all keyed up but a date, you might have a beer or glass of wine to take the edge off. These are a few of the many coping strategies you can use *after* the anxiety is experienced.

Current research into the interplay between anxiety and emotion regulation points to strong evidence that interventional strategies such as reappraisal can build one's capacity for emotion regulation and positively affect anxiety; these studies have been done in the context of anxiety disorders.[7] Specifically, neuroimaging studies have shown that negative emotions of anxiety or fear lessen in response to emotion regulation strategies. Further, neuroimaging studies have also shown that the negative emotions of anxiety or fear occur in different neural regions of the brain from where emotion regulation occurs. This area of research is in its infancy, with many research questions driving its expansion. But this is good news: We can update our emotional responses. We can learn to emotionally regulate. We can become better at managing and then channeling our anxiety.

I like to think of this approach to anxiety as a way of building our resilience to stress. In Chapter Four we will do a deep dive into how anxiety's brain-body pathways can enhance our overall resilience—physical and emotional—but for now, consider this: We need to both feel the feelings and update our responses to those feelings. This begins with awareness. Once you realize you get uncomfortable at any sign of anxiety, you need to stop and think about what you do with the feelings. We all need constant practice simply sitting with our feelings, sitting with the discomfort, and not trying to immediately mask, deny, escape, or distract ourselves. By simply sitting with the discomfort, you do two things: You get accustomed to the feeling and realize that you can indeed "survive" it, and you give yourself time and space in your brain to make a more conscious decision about how to act or respond. This is exactly how a new, more positive neural pathway is established.

3

Coping with Anxiety in Real Life

In the face of stressors and the anxiety they often trigger, we all develop coping strategies to manage and get ourselves back on track—that state of equilibrium where we feel comfortable and grounded. This is to stay that we naturally try to regulate our emotions and bounce back when we are knocked off course. These go-to behaviors or thought processes become conditioned responses lodged in our memories; in other words, they often function automatically, beneath our conscious awareness.

But many of these strategies were developed when we were younger and less mindful. For example, at seven years old a girl who felt afraid of the dark may have resorted to rocking or hiding under her bed covers. At seventeen, she may still wish she could resort to rocking when she gets afraid, but now she is embarrassed by this habit so instead she drinks a beer or smokes some weed to numb the discomfort of her feelings. Instead of updating the way she handles being afraid of the dark, this young woman has created a maladaptive coping strategy that can lead to more negative consequences down the road.

Some people take sleeping medication to knock themselves out. Some people self-soothe using comfort objects—for the vast majority of adults, phones have taken the place of lovies or binkies. What I often find myself doing when pressured by a deadline is eating more. Although none of these behaviors are harmful in small doses, you can imagine that if a person relied on them repeatedly, problems could arise—as they did for me a decade or so ago when I gained twenty-five pounds.

Coping mechanisms are essentially behaviors or actions we develop to self-soothe or avoid an uncomfortable feeling. When these coping mechanisms stop working to manage the stress, they tend to make matters worse, exacerbating our anxiety and undermining our belief that we are in control of our lives. In general, coping mechanisms are considered to be either adaptive (i.e., good at helping us manage the stress) or maladaptive (bad for us because they cause other damage—either through avoiding a problem that only gets bigger or giving us another problem, as is the case with alcohol dependence or abuse).

The boy who got into fights in the schoolyard when he felt threatened at eight years old may still lash out angrily as an adult if he senses the need to defend himself; perhaps this occurs on the subway when someone jostles him getting on or off. The young woman who discovered cutting as a way to mitigate her inner loneliness may still, at thirty, be unable to find positive ways of soothing her fears and insecurities and so has moved on to bulimia. For a time, these behaviors help dull the pain at the base of the negative emotions—the pent-up anger or the dire sense of isolation or the fear of the dark. But when the feelings underneath these behaviors are left untouched or unprocessed, those components of anxiety will grow and stay stuck; the negative coping behaviors only reinforce the inability to manage or regulate the feelings.

Here's another example.

RALPH: AN EXAMPLE OF A POOR COPING STRATEGY

Ralph has a thirty-minute commute to and from work every day. He is having a hard time at his job; there are a lot of internal politics that are wearing him down and fraying his last nerve. When he gets in his car on a Friday at 5:15 p.m. he is particularly anxious to get home, have a beer, and relax in front of the TV. He's hoping there's a good game on that will distract and relax him.

But as he pulls onto the freeway he's met with heavy traffic. Everyone is in a rush it seems but there's little room to move. Ralph begins to change lanes. His temper is rising and when a young guy in a pickup truck cuts him off, Ralph just loses it. He becomes enraged, speeds up, and swerves dangerously close to the pickup so the driver can get an eyeful of his gesticulating and an earful of his horn that he is leaning on. He's got a hair-trigger temper he just can't control.

From our point of view, it may seem like Ralph had some options before he blasted his horn and swerved to make his feelings known, but after years of letting road rage run free, there's little time or space in his brain for a different reaction: without even thinking, Ralph explodes with rage. His anger is unprocessed; the neural pathway from stimuli to response is just too strongly ingrained. And yet, he still has the potential to "unlearn" this behavior.

At this point in time, Ralph's response shows that he is emotionally dysregulated and has very little, if any, control over his reactions. The intensity of his negative emotion has been reinforced again and again, provoking similar types of reactions to the road rage. However, with repeated exposure to positive tools to manage his emotions, Ralph could learn not only to more effectively manage his reaction to the traffic but also ways to more constructively cope with his situation at work. He could also benefit from some help preparing for his commute, such as having a conscious wind-down practice before he gets in his car. But without ever taking a step back and giving himself space to consider what he might like to change, Ralph will continue to reinforce the stress and anxiety patterns.

Chronic maladaptation to stress affects our brains and bodies in numerous ways, at numerous levels, including the neuroendocrine system, the autonomic nervous system, and the cardiovascular and immune systems.[1]

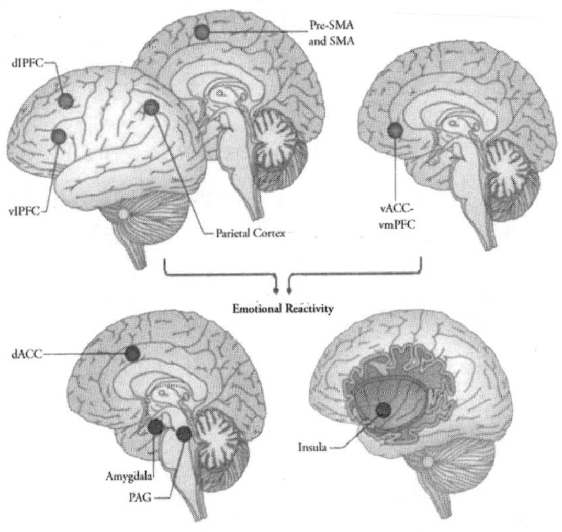

Figure 3. **Brain areas implicated in emotional regulation.** Emotional arousal (i.e., your panic attack) is processed in the amygdala and basal ganglia and relayed to the ventrolateral prefrontal cortex (VLPFC), the anterior insula, the supplementary motor area (SMA), the angular gyrus, and the superior temporal gyrus (STG). Emotional appraisal is started in the VLPFC, which signals the need to regulate emotions to the dorsolateral prefrontal cortex (DLPFC). The DLPFC processes emotional regulation and sends signals to the angular gyrus, the SMA, the STG, the amgydala, and the basal ganglia that help regulate the unwanted emotional state. Figure reproduced with permission Etkin et al., 2015.

· POSITIVE AND NEGATIVE COPING ACTIONS ·

We develop coping strategies to manage our negative emotions. They are behaviors and actions that help us mitigate or redirect our discomfort, fear, pain, and so on. And for this reason, our coping strategies often reflect our relationship to anxiety. If you cope in ways that are productive for you, then you probably have your anxiety under control. If you cope with stress in ways that undermine your health, job, safety, or relationships to your loved ones, it may be time to consider your options.

It's important to become more aware of how we respond to stress and feelings of anxiety. The use of more than two or three negative coping strategies can be an indication of being stuck in bad anxiety; on the other hand, use of positive coping strategies shows a tolerance of stress and flexibility around emotions.

Consider the list below. Ask yourself if any of them are familiar to you. Don't judge yourself; simply take note.

Negative Coping Actions

- use or abuse alcohol or drugs
- act violently toward others (verbally, physically, sexually, or emotionally)
- act out or misbehave on purpose
- avoid conflict
- rationalize or blame others for your problems
- deny there is a problem
- repress or forget what has happened
- behave like someone you are not
- disassociate self from situation
- exhibit controlling behavior
- become a workaholic (stay busy to avoid your feelings)
- self-harm; think about or attempt suicide
- isolate yourself and withdraw from activities and others

- feel like you need to control or manipulate others
- refuse to communicate
- fantasize regularly
- catastrophize
- be overly helpful (help others over self)

Next, go through the list of positive coping mechanisms; these are considered adaptive because they are beneficial ways of managing anxiety.

Positive Coping Actions

- name your feelings, whether positive or negative
- control anger—neither suffocating it nor letting rage take over
- practice self-reflection
- seek support from friends and family
- communicate or talk about feelings
- exercise (exercise has been shown to dampen anxiety)
    - stay sexually active (sex is known to reduce anxiety and quiet the nervous system)
- participate in hobbies (such as beadwork) and/or sports
- spend time outdoors
- consider the situation from another point of view
- remain flexible and open to new ways of thinking
- keep a journal or other form of conscious self-reflection
- spend quality time with family, partner, friends
- use positive self-talk and affirmations
- meditate or pray
- clean or organize your workspace or home
- seek support from a health professional when you are ill
- play with a pet or children

· WHEN COPING WITH ANXIETY STOPS WORKING ·

Our relationship with anxiety likely changes over time, as does our ability to process it. Coping strategies necessarily have to be updated and ones that are maladaptive need to be addressed. And sometimes this process requires some work.

LIZA: WHERE DID MY GROOVE GO?

Liza is a hard-driving career woman. A graduate of Harvard Business School, she dove into a career in financial services, showed wicked smarts, social intelligence, and is well liked and well respected by her colleagues. She's been on the fast track for more than ten years and suddenly she's forty-one with no life outside of work. She's a workaholic, and up until now all of this dedication and motivation to succeed has paid dividends—not just to her bank account but also to her sense of self-worth. But lately she goes home to her beautifully appointed Back Bay apartment feeling totally burned-out. She drinks three to four glasses of wine to relax and help herself fall asleep, without realizing how terrible alcohol is for her overall sleep quality. Her alarm gets her up at 5 a.m. so she can run along the Charles River and make it to the office by 7 a.m. This is her cycle and it has worked for her for years, but not anymore. Liza now wakes in the morning already feeling depleted. She is lonely, plagued with self-doubt, and beginning to question what is driving her so hard.

Liza is used to worrying; it's what always helped motivate her to work harder and longer than any of her colleagues. She got a lot of positive feedback for her industriousness, and she took this to heart. In other words, she used to be able to direct the high activation of her anxiety circuits for good.

But over the last couple of years, especially after she passed her fortieth birthday, she's been realizing that she no longer gets the high from work or the satisfaction from being well regarded by her boss and colleagues. When she's at work, she's consumed, but outside of work she has become almost paralyzed. What is she worried about? That she is alone, that she is getting older, that she will no longer be considered a bright young star at work.

She has begun to feel that her nervous energy is seeping out of her, no longer under her control. The only way she thinks she can dull the emotional discomfort is through wine at the end of the day—even looking ahead to her glass of wine gets her through moments when she feels so much stress at work that it is like her head is going to explode. She is still running every morning but it's no longer enjoyable; it's become a dreaded habit. She feels like she's running for her life and away from her fears: fear of getting fat, fear of slowing down, fear about what will happen when or if she stops running.

If Liza were able to stop and take a closer look at her patterns, she'd notice some red flags: her energy has waned, she no longer feels excited about work, she feels increasingly agitated. These brain-body changes are indications of worsening anxiety. Liza may not yet have clinical anxiety, but her bad anxiety is becoming increasingly intense and more frequent, taking a toll on her, which shows that her coping mechanisms are no longer keeping her anxiety at bay.

A scan of Liza's brain would likely reveal high activation in both the amygdala and the part of the frontal lobe called the dorsal anterior cingulate cortex, which are typically activated in states of anxiety. Liza's adaptive behaviors that once kept these brain activations in balance seem to be having less of an effect. Even worse, these same behaviors have now become maladaptive: The vigilant exercise, the seeking out of positive feedback and compliments from her boss and colleagues, and the "downtime" in the form of a few glasses of wine used to take the edge off her anxiety enough to relax, recharge, and tap into her ambition to achieve. It's hard to say when things started to change. As we know, chronic stress depletes important neurotransmitters, interrupts sleep, and degrades the adrenals—all of which we need to keep us emotionally regulated (i.e., in physical and emotional balance, also called homeostasis). And there's never one cause for why anxiety that was once manageable and helpful becomes problematic.

But Liza has some choices to make: She can continue the same behaviors, reinforcing the maladaptive coping, *or* she can take steps to do things differently. Before she does anything, however, she needs to believe she has the power to change. Liza must take ownership of her ability to decide, to act, and to believe that she is in more control of her situation than she currently feels, and even probably imagines.

It's more than likely that Liza's brain is in the midst of a negative type of adaptation. The longer she stays unaware of how her coping mechanisms are no longer benefiting her or giving her the mental break she needs, the more intense her bad anxiety and the more entrenched her negative coping strategies will become. But once she is able to see her situation for what it truly is—a case of an overdue update to her coping strategies—Liza will be able to start changing aspects of her situation that will allow her to orient herself to a more satisfying life.

Here's another example of coping mechanisms no longer working.

JARED: HELP, I'M NOT SURE WHAT TO DO WITH MY LIFE

When I met Jared he was twenty-six years old, five years out of college. He'd been living with his parents, unable to figure out what he wanted to do. His parents worried about him: No job seemed good enough or interesting enough for him. He'd been to a headhunter, he'd worked with a career coach. He was overcome with anxiety about what to do with his life and couldn't commit to trying an entry-level position at a small company, a medium-size company, or any company at all. Jared was contemplating going to graduate school, but he had no passion for any particular subject and he certainly didn't want to get himself into debt. His parents had already told him they would not foot the bill.

His parents were frustrated with him, annoyed that they'd spent so much on tuition only for him to appear so unable to make a plan for his future. His parents were also annoyed with themselves, feeling as if they were enabling Jared's inability to make a decision or move. They wondered if they should just kick him out so he would feel more compelled to get a job, any job.

Jared was actually terrified.

With each passing week and month, he seemed ever more stuck in a kind of paralysis with no motivation, no confidence, no energy. He overate (and gained about twenty pounds), and he stopped reaching out to friends (they were busy with their new jobs or starting new relationships). Jared's anxiety had become so bad that he was completely at a standstill, unable to make a decision that could change his circumstances.

Now let me address one point here: Jared was not only suffering from acute anxiety but also long-term depression. Anxiety and depression are overlapping conditions that often occur together and share many of the same neurobiological characteristics, such as a dysregulation of or imbalance between serotonin and dopamine, and a stress response that is dysfunctional. Jared was not always depressed, but he had always been anxious; now, his anxiety had gone on so long that it had triggered depression. At a neurochemical level, he was suffering from what doctors call dysthymia or persistent depressive disorder (PDD), a long-term or chronic depression. But this situation could have been avoided if Jared had known that he could actually harness his anxiety—that his constant and growing nervous energy could have been directed toward a problem instead of away from it. Had Jared acted more quickly to address his anxious feelings postgraduation, and if he had remained socially and physically active, his anxiety may not have spilled over and triggered depression. The relationship between anxiety and depression is complex, and there is no one way to predict how any individual will express a neurochemical imbalance.

Yet we do know that these two conditions—while they seem like opposites—often coexist.

Liza's and Jared's situations not only show vividly how our behaviors impact our emotional states and vice versa but also how everyday bad anxiety can creep into our lives, steal our energy and focus, and sap us of motivation and well-being. Liza and Jared may not have had clinical disorders but their lives were being disrupted by their bad anxiety. Like all of us, they naturally developed strategies to manage their emotions and anxiety. For Jared, his withdrawal from others and avoidance of challenge gave some relief to his fears about his future. The trouble with this coping strategy was that, over time, the withdrawal and avoidance exacerbated his anxiety and made him feel even more alone and helpless. The coping mechanism that might have been useful in the short term ended up pushing his anxiety even deeper into the bad zone and triggering depression. Jared was at a scary time in life; he was done with a successful and fun college career and now faced choices in the real world for the first time. He felt completely inadequate. And unfortunately, the coping mechanisms he was reaching for were only making those feelings worse.

Liza was also entering a different phase of life. She was no longer the scrappy "new kid on the block," so she was being forced to adapt her work goals to this new, more "advanced" time in her career. As her anxiety increased, Liza increasingly relied on alcohol to cope with the discomfort of her feelings. At first her stalwart coping mechanisms (exercise and wine) took the edge off her anxiety so she could rest, relax, and reset during the evening and be ready to roll the next day. But her increasing use of alcohol began creating secondary problems—sleep disruption as well as hangovers—that clouded her thinking and decision making and caused a deterioration in her physical energy and enthusiasm. Liza's coping techniques were no longer helping her anxiety; the alcohol, in particular, was exacerbating it, making things worse.

....

Our brains work automatically to create strategies for avoiding unpleasant feelings (such as anxiety) and masking their severity. This avoidance is built into our neural pathways and wiring and helps us manage stress and keep going. But as our internal and external lives/environments change, we often outgrow these coping mechanisms or they just stop working. We may or may not realize this shift in their efficacy. Typically, however, there's some evidence of the habit getting in our way instead of helping us: Liza began to drink too many glasses of wine; Jared's depression and anxiety kept him avoidant of anything remotely challenging, rendering him frozen in the face of decision making. These are signs that their anxiety shifted back from good to bad, manageable to unmanageable.

To better understand how this happens, it can help to take a look at what is actually happening in the body when bad anxiety takes the wheel. In short:

- Physical under-activation/depletion manifests in different ways. When your brain-body is under chronic strain from anxiety, your capacity to manage emotions becomes downregulated (i.e., less effective at responding to internal or external stimuli). You become highly sensitive to stress of any kind and can begin to feel self-doubts and a loss of confidence.
- Then, when your body is depleted and doesn't get enough restorative time and rest, it will not be able to kick up your motivation, the predominant emotion of a positive mindset. This inability to reset further erodes the capacity to maintain emotion regulation.
- If you then isolate yourself, you remove the opportunity for encouragement and support from social relationships and thereby take away a vital bad-anxiety buffer.

- Further, if you look to drugs or alcohol for relief, you may unintentionally exacerbate your anxiety once the "high" has passed. Indeed, drugs and alcohol act as a depressant on the nervous system. They also interfere with the brain-body's processing of dopamine and serotonin, giving you a false sense of relief from anxiety.

These responses represent a downregulation in functioning of various neural pathways of the brain-body. And yet for all these negative coping strategies and their drawbacks, a silver lining can emerge: It is entirely possible to change not only current ways of coping with negative emotion and anxiety but also the underlying effects on the brain-body. Restoring emotion regulation requires energy, curiosity, and recognizing that you have a choice. But it is absolutely possible for any of us to learn to recognize signs of our own physical depletion and/or emotional dysregulation and begin to make changes. This is the essence of how using good anxiety works, and it all comes down to the brain's plasticity.

When we understand how these underlying pathways trigger, reinforce, or redirect anxiety's arousal, then we can combat bad anxiety and make conscious decisions that enable us to steer our own path. When we learn to cue in to our own feelings, thoughts, and behaviors, not only can we shift from bad to good anxiety but we can shift our energy, attitude, mindset, and intentions. We will be able to jump-start, reshape, or boost our motivation in all sectors of life—body, mind, and relationships. All of us can create the life we truly want by allocating all our resources in positive, empowering ways that help us achieve our goals and manifest our dreams.

Just like anxiety itself, all of our experience, behaviors, feelings, thoughts, decisions, and mental constructs (e.g., perceptions and interpretations) are based in part on how our brain-bodies are functioning physiologically (how our bodies respond to any kind of stimuli), mentally (cognition and our thought processes), emotionally (our feelings and core emotional states that are both unconscious and conscious), and socially (how our relationships and social situations impact our biology).

By reframing the way you think about anxiety, you can take what was once a major drag and turn it into something useful and even beneficial in your life. And as you achieve this flip, you will naturally open the door to the extraordinary benefits that anxiety is designed to bring into your life. When functioning properly, anxiety can essentially grant you six superpowers: the ability to strengthen your overall physical and emotional resilience; perform tasks and activities at a higher level; optimize your mindset; increase your focus and productivity; enhance your social intelligence; and improve your creative skills. Getting a handle on your anxiety and shifting it to good opens the door to discovering how anxiety can become a superpower.

Throughout Part Two you will discover six pathways of anxiety you can use to open the door to your own refresh in your relation to anxiety. The six pathways or "neural networks" (groups of functionally related brain areas) include the emotion or attitude network, the attention network (including that top-down regulatory network I have been referring to), the connection network (related to the pathways of our social brain), the reward or motivation network, the creativity network, and the resilience network (related to our built-in drive to survive). All these brain networks overlap and interact with one another, sharing neural pathways and signaling one another in a constant, dynamic way.

PART TWO

Learning How to Worry Well: Anxiety's Hidden Superpowers

4

Supercharge Your Resilience

Managing anxiety and ultimately transforming it for a different, better purpose comes down to resilience. All the brain networks we've discussed offer gateways to either calming anxious thoughts and feelings or utilizing the energy, arousal, and discomfort to be better, do better, and feel better. This is the essence of resilience.

Resilience is the ability to adapt and recover from hardship in our lives. We need resilience every day to help us through challenges, disappointments, real or perceived insults, or any situation that might feel painful. It's also one of the most important tools we have to draw from in the face of loss, sorrow, or trauma. Traumatic events call upon us to survive; they pull on every last ounce of our strength and emotional and physical resources.

In other words, we rely on resilience all the time. And just as we are wired for survival, we are also wired for resilience. Indeed, the adaptiveness that comes with our brain plasticity sets us up to be resilient and flexible, and to bounce back after setbacks. As a scientist I think of resilience as successful adaptation and the ability to effectively respond to the stressors in our lives. And the good news is that in spite of the inevitability of these stressors—both big and small—we can learn to build our resilience. We build resilience by learning how to think flexibly and accepting that we are not defined by our failures. We build resilience by acknowledging what we need and knowing when to ask for help. We also build resilience when we seek out pleasure and sources of enjoyment, from food to sports to sex. Yes, having fun helps build our stores of resilience!

When we challenge ourselves and grow more confident, we build our resilience. When we figure out how to dial down our body's stress response through relaxation techniques, we build our resilience. When we eat right, get enough sleep, and exercise, we boost our physical resilience and in turn, support our psychological resilience. In essence, because our brain-bodies are wired to adapt, we can build resilience of brain, body, and mind. When confronted with setbacks, failure, or sadness we can actively choose to find opportunities to optimize our stress response. Sometimes this entails revisiting coping strategies that are maladaptive (i.e., that aggravate anxiety and cause other problems). Resilience is not an either/or. It is not only a dynamic system of interacting brain-body signals that protects us as a survival mechanism by coming to our rescue in the hardest of times but is also a daily awareness, energy, and resourcefulness that we actively cultivate and strengthen.

It should be no surprise that anxiety can weaken our resilience; chronic hypervigilance, rage, fear, and relentless worry wear us down physically, emotionally, and spiritually. It takes away our strength, courage, and immunity, depleting us of our emotional and physical reserves. However, as we've seen, when we pay attention and act on anxiety's protective signal from deep within us, we are motivated to take care of ourselves, seek safety, surround ourselves with trustworthy people, and be brave enough to separate from people who hurt us. Resilience can be a conscious, deliberate choice.

The true power of resilience is that it emanates from our own personal smorgasbord of both successes *and failures* as they gradually build over our entire lifetime. Resilience also builds from leaning on our adaptive coping strategies, the ones we know and rely on to get us through those tough days and stressful situations when anxiety can hit. Actually, dear readers, resilience is full circle to *one of the most powerful* abilities that everyday anxiety affords us: the power to build our own personal and replenishable source of resilience in our lives. Anxiety helps build up our resilience stores; anxiety also alerts us to the need for recovery and self-care. In neuroscience, we call it stress inoculation.[1]

· THE CATCH-22 OF STRESS AND RESILIENCE ·

Stress and resilience go together like yin and yang. The American Psychological Association defines *resilience* as "the process of adapting well in the face of adversity, trauma, tragedy, threats, or significant sources of stress."[2] By this definition, resilience would not exist if there was no challenge, stress, or hardship in our lives. In neurobiological terms, resilience is the outcome of how we manage stress each and every day and over our entire lifetime. In 1915, Walter Bradford Cannon[3] first identified resilience as the "visceral adaptive response to different stimuli." In his lab at Harvard, he observed how the body changed in response to such stressors as hunger, cold, exercise, and strong emotions. This early work led Cannon to be the first to identify the fight-or-flight response to stress. A few years later, he coined the term "homeostasis" to describe the body's drive to maintain a "dynamic equilibrium."

This research has grown and evolved since the early 1900s, and we now know a lot more about the stress response system. In an oversimplified way, we can think about the stress response as having two major pathways that correspond to two phases.

The first phase of our stress response will be very familiar to you from Chapter One (page 20). It involves activation of the sympathetic "fight-or-flight" (autonomic) nervous system. You will recall that this is when your brain-body becomes alert, vigilant, and appraises whether there is a real or potential threat and also triggers an automatic cascade of physiological changes, including energy mobilization, metabolic changes, activation of the immune system, and suppression of the digestive and reproductive systems.

The second phase is slower and longer lasting, and the most familiar element at this stage is the release of the "stress hormone" cortisol through the hypothalamic-pituitary-adrenal (HPA) axis. In parallel with the release of cortisol is that of a wide range of other powerful hormones we now know coincide with the release of a large network of powerful neurotransmitters that also help regulate our response to stress. For example, the neurotransmitter neuropeptide Y (NPY): This critical neurotransmitter you have probably never heard of is famous for counteracting the anxiety-producing effects of cortisol. Galanin, another neurotransmitter that gets into the mix, has been shown to decrease anxiety. Dopamine release in areas associated with the feelings of reward decreases in stress and anxiety; and serotonin has a complex relationship with stress and anxiety, increasing those responses when it is released in some areas of the brain and decreasing their levels when released in others.

Some scientists have focused on allostatic load or overload as a way to understand how well the stress system is working to manage outside stressors. Regardless of which terminology is used, scientists are in agreement that physical and psychological stress is processed by a complex and interactive set of circuits in the brain. Sometimes the load/overload is managed well and homeostasis is achieved, but sometimes the overload wins.

Most of our understanding of how resilience is built or weakened comes from research into extreme conditions like PTSD and trauma. For example, studies of early-childhood trauma often note the presence of a highly sensitive sympathetic-adreno-medullary (SAM) axis, which has also been tied to both an enlarged amygdala as well as a smaller hippocampus. The amygdala is the part of the brain that detects threat; the hippocampus, which is the key brain area critical to our ability to form and retain new long-term memories, is what helps us *appraise* the threat. A smaller hippocampus suggests that the ability to accurately appraise threat is diminished. These anatomical differences have not only been reported in people who have experienced childhood trauma but also in those with PTSD. These findings have also been supported by extensive research using monkeys, including studies of monkeys in the wild showing how males that are lowest in the hierarchy and therefore get last choice for food and mating partners show signs of chronic stress including smaller hippocampi.[4]

While we still don't have all the answers, we have made progress in understanding some of the major biological, psychological, and environmental factors that either tip some vulnerable people over into clinical depression/anxiety/PTSD or that enable others to withstand even greater suffering, manage the experience, and recover a sense of well-being. The continuing research also points to psychobiological differences that seem to predict stronger resilience in some people based on genetic makeup (neurochemistry). For instance, people who have disruptions in either the production or regulation of dopamine, one of the central neurotransmitters that modulate the reward system of the brain, can become more prone to anxiety, depression, and addictive illness. Epigenetic factors such as how a person's lifestyle impacts their brain functioning can also make someone more susceptible to anxiety and lessen one's overall psychological and physical resilience. A depleted or compromised immune system is another example of a weakened physical resilience that can also have psychological effects. For example, people with autoimmune disorders such as fibromyalgia have a higher incidence of depression; their ability to fend off low moods is weakened by the overall depressed state of their immune system.

Again, much of our thinking about and studying of resilience has concerned that which occurs as a response to trauma or abuse. But when we ask the questions—How is it that some of us seem, after setbacks, to have an easier time bouncing back than others? How is it that some who experience tragedy and trauma, especially those who go through this early in life, suffer more long-term damage, including anxiety disorders, major depressive disorder (MDD), and posttraumatic stress disorder (PTSD)?—we can identify, and scientists have begun to investigate, the characteristics of resilience so that we can learn not only how to respond better after tragic events, losses, or other forms of trauma but also how to grow the seeds of resilience before we need it. Just as preventative medicine acts as a way to avoid disease and offset aging, building resilience before we necessarily need it is not just a safety measure but a route to living a healthier, more balanced life.

Scientists have also tried to isolate biological factors that indicate resilience. For instance, studies have shown that higher levels of NPY are often associated with resilience; studies have shown that NPY produces calming effects and counteracts the anxiety-producing effects of cortisol; studies have shown that soldiers who withstood traumatic events without developing unshakable PTSD tended to have higher levels of NPY. But we need a balance of NPY and cortisol for a healthy stress response. Too much or too little of either will offset homeostasis. Also, brain-derived neurotrophic factor (BDNF), a growth factor essential for the growth and function of the hippocampus, critical for long-term memory and also stimulated by physical aerobic exercise, has been implicated in resilience.[5]

· TOXIC STRESS, TRAUMA, AND RESILIENCE ·

It is well established that early experiences of adversity, including maltreatment, can precipitate a range of psychological and social problems that extend across one's lifetime. Individuals who have experienced childhood abuse are at greater risk for posttraumatic stress disorder,[6] anxiety,[7] depression,[8] substance abuse,[9] and antisocial behavior.[10] Specifically, neuroendocrine studies have demonstrated that experiences of early adversity can alter the functioning of the hypothalamic-pituitary-adrenal (HPA) axis, which is associated with more sensitivity to environmental stressors such as air-pollution and food insecurity.[11] Research has demonstrated structural brain differences associated with childhood abuse.[12,13]

Harvard professor Dr. Jack Shonkoff has long studied this area of research at the Center on the Developing Child at Harvard's Chan School of Public Health.[14] He has defined three possible ways we can respond to stress: positive, tolerable, and toxic. As described below, these terms refer to the stress response system's effects on the body, not to the stressful event or experience itself:

- A **positive stress response** is our built-in biopsychosocial skills that enable us to deal with daily stressors. Indeed, this positive stress response is akin to how we've been characterizing good anxiety—a brief increase in heart rate and mild elevations in hormone levels.
- A **tolerable stress response** is marked by an activation of the body's inner alarm system provoked by a truly frightening or dangerous encounter, the death of a loved one, or a big romantic breakup or divorce. During such intense stress, the brain-body can offset the impact through conscious self-care, such as turning to a support system. The key here is that the

person's resilience factor is already stable enough to enable the recovery. If, for instance, someone is faced with a life crisis and they don't have a strong resilience factor, then they will be less able to recover and bounce back.

- A **toxic stress response** occurs when a child or adult undergoes ongoing or prolonged adversity—such as poverty, abject neglect, physical or emotional abuse, chronic neglect, exposure to violence—without sufficient support in place. This kind of prolonged activation of the stress response systems can not only disrupt the development of brain architecture and other organ systems of the child but also lingers well into adulthood, robbing people of their ability to manage any kind of stress.

When a heightened stress response occurs continually, or is triggered by multiple sources, it can take a cumulative toll on an individual's physical and mental health—for a lifetime. The more adverse experiences in childhood, the greater the likelihood of developmental delays and later health problems, including heart disease, diabetes, substance abuse, and depression. Toxic stress is associated with anxiety disorders, aggressive behavior, a lack of cognitive flexibility, and lower IQ.[15] Other researchers have found that prolonged perceived stress is associated with a reduced hippocampal volume, making this structure even more vulnerable to anxiety, age-related cognitive decline, as well as health problems such as diabetes, MDD, Cushing's disease, and PTSD.[16] As mentioned above, the hippocampus is the brain structure critical to our ability to form and retain new memories of facts and events and is one of the most vulnerable structures in aging and dementia, including Alzheimer's disease. Not only does prolonged stress affect your ability to form and retain new long-term memories but it can literally start to damage the cells of the hippocampus, making them shrink and thereby more vulnerable to age-related cognitive decline. In these cases, there is no good amount of chronic stress.

· STRESS INOCULATION AND DEVELOPING ACTIVE COPING STRATEGIES ·

You may recall from Chapter Three that our first line of defense in managing any kind of stress is through coping strategies. These strategies offer us ways to measure our ability to manage stress; whether these are adaptive (i.e., helpful) or maladaptive (harmful) says a lot about our resilience capacity. Some neurobiologists refer to our coping strategies in other ways, such as the contrasting active and passive coping responses. Active coping responses are "intentional efforts of the subject aimed at minimizing the physical, psychological, or social harm of a stressor" and imply an attempt to gain "control" over the stressor. Passive coping, which refers to avoidance or "learned helplessness,"[17] occurs when a person avoids a stressful situation but also avoids building resilience to the stressor. In such cases, the individual becomes more vulnerable or susceptible to the impact of stress and therefore is considered less resilient.

Studies of early-childhood stress showed that early exposure to uncontrollable stressful situations (aka, situations of war or childhood abuse) can lead to what scientists call learned helplessness.[18] This is when children learn that nothing they do will change their stressful situation, and the outcome is often a long-term pathology, including PTSD and depression. The long-term negative consequences of learned helplessness have been studied extensively in rodents. Interestingly, scientists discovered that if you expose rats to the same number of stressful situations and give them the opportunity to remove, avoid, escape, or control a stressor (i.e., use an active coping strategy) not only did these rats *not* exhibit PTSD-like symptoms but instead they developed a higher than average resilience to subsequent stressful situations. Scientists have called this response stress inoculation, and it has not only been studied and confirmed in rodents and monkeys but also shown to work for humans as well.[19]

What the science of stress inoculation tells us is that we are all born with tools to get ourselves out of the stress/anxiety-provoking situation. Just to be clear, all anxiety-provoking situations will engage your stress response, but the act of exercising those responses helps inoculate you from future stress/anxiety responses. It is as if you are teaching yourself that you *CAN* survive these situations, and the better you get at first feeling that anxiety and then acting to mitigate the stress response, the better you will manage in the future. In a sense, this gives you the opportunity to retrain your stress response with every anxiety-provoking situation you encounter as long as you are aware of your options and tools to flip that bad-anxiety response to a good one.

When I realized the power of using current anxiety to help inoculate us against future anxiety, it made me want to create a Fitbit for emotions. Wouldn't it be great to have a device that didn't count steps but instead gave you a stress inoculation score based on how you were able to avoid or lessen a stressful situation? I think this score would be a fantastic motivating tool that would be like a big high five to all of us battling bad anxiety and veering closer to learned helplessness than stress inoculation. While we don't have that "Stressbit" yet, try to keep a running total of your successful anxiety interventions and be your own anxiety coach and give yourself a high five as those numbers AND your stress/anxiety inoculation go up!

· BUILDING RESILIENCE ·

Multiple studies have shown that we can actively build our resilience and sometimes even reverse deleterious effects of trauma on our stress system. Scientists continue to explore the negative impacts of prolonged stress; they are also looking at what is happening when people are able to avoid or resist the deleterious effects—essentially, what it takes for people to become more resilient in ways that protect the brain and overall health.

Indeed, in a review of the neuroscience of resilience studies, Gang Wu[20] and colleagues identified numerous characteristics that have been associated with people who show strong resilience. What's particularly exciting is that most of these characteristics align with the anxiety superpowers:

1) An optimistic outlook (often referred to as having a positive affect) has been shown to reduce negative mood and anxiety and quicken recovery from traumatic events. Although I'm not suggesting you can generate an optimistic outlook out of thin air, we do know that it can be developed over time. Studies have shown how an optimistic attitude goes hand in hand with overall well-being, good physical health, and having a strong social network. This optimistic, flexible way of thinking is the basis of the activist mindset superpower (see Chapter Six).

2) Cognitive flexibility and reappraisal, two fundamental aspects of emotion regulation, can also be learned, practiced, and ultimately used as a form of psychological resilience. As we will see in our discussion of how the attention network can be hijacked by anxiety (see Chapter Seven), cognitive flexibility enables us to recruit our attention, refocus, and resist internalizing failures as indications of who we are. This cognitive

nimbleness helps pivot your anxiety and becomes a form of psychological resilience.

3) Social support, which entails seeking out loving or caring relationships to help buffer the impact of stress, is indeed a superpower of anxiety. The importance of our relationships, our ability to empathize, and ultimately our ability to show compassion buffer against anxiety; this very buffer is a form of resilience.

4) Humor has been shown to be an active way to lessen anxiety and tension brought on by stress and has been shown to help people build both physical and psychological resilience.

5) Physical exercise not only improves our overall health and brain-body functioning but also acts as a source of physiological resilience, helping us manage stress both physically and psychologically.

6) Altruism, or what scientists refer to as "prosocial behavior," has been shown to promote recovery from trauma. I see this resilience booster as an extension of the superpower of compassion, which helps us fuel a stronger connection to our fellow human beings and goes a long way toward offsetting anxiety and making us more emotionally resilient.

7) Mindfulness as a conscious practice, including meditation, yoga, and other mindful activities, has been shown to reduce passive or avoidant coping, such as reliance on alcohol, in response to stress. In this way, a mindfulness practice is

> like a prophylactic against anxiety and depression and it in turn builds psychological resilience.

Stress is not only an inevitable fact of our lives but also something we are designed to deal with; in fact, stress is what forces us to adapt, learn, and evolve, both as individuals and a species. The cliché is true: All of the most important life lessons come from the challenges we face and how we deal with them. The key point here is that resilience comes not only from the confidence and self-belief that we gain from the successes in our lives but, perhaps more importantly, from surviving, adjusting, and moving on after the inevitable failures and challenges. It takes both sides of this equation to build our superpower of resilience. We need to go through hard things in order to know we can survive them.

No matter how resilient we are, there will always be experiences that test us. I had one such time in my life that tested me and my resilience.

· *MY STORY* ·

The moment is clear as day: It was a cool and cloudy early Monday morning in May, and I was enjoying waking up in my New York City apartment after a weeklong trip to Minnesota where I had given three talks and spent the weekend happily shopping at one of the biggest pottery festivals that region offers. I was in the middle of my regular morning tea meditation that I do to center myself. I had my plan: Later that day, I was going to dive into draft number one of the first chapter of this book.

It was the last days of the spring semester and I was super busy. I was wrapping up an upper-division neuroscience lab class for honors students, preparing to chair the last promotion and tenure meeting of the year, writing papers, supervising research, and, most urgently, putting the finishing touches on the commencement speech I was invited to give by our dean at that year's baccalaureate ceremony for the College of Arts and Sciences at New York University to be held at Radio City Music Hall in just a few days' time. Pushing myself through my various deadlines is a familiar task for me, one that I'm good at—persevering, working hard and diligently to meet deadlines, and using the stress of it all to help drive me forward. I was just a few drafts away from finishing my speech and then right after my address, the academic year would be officially over and my calendar would suddenly open up and expand like a colorful New York City pop-up book, which would allow me to deeply engage in the creative process and nitty-gritty neuroscience research for this, my second book.

But then, out of nowhere, the unimaginable happened.

At six thirty that morning my cell phone rang. It was my brother's business colleague from Shanghai, who told me that my younger brother and only sibling, David, had suffered a major heart attack and died. Just shy of his fifty-first birthday, my brother was suddenly, irretrievably gone.

David was a businessman, investor, and entrepreneur and had been living and building his own company in Shanghai for the last few years while commuting back and forth to California to spend quality time with his family. I had seen my brother most recently when we had both flown back to the West Coast to be with our mom when our father had passed away just three months earlier. In his last years, my dad had suffered from dementia, and his death (also from a sudden heart attack), painful as it was, was not totally unexpected. I had imagined and prepared myself for what it might be like if/when we lost Dad. But David? His death was unfathomable.

Those first few hours after I got the news were surreal. I felt disconnected from reality. My world had suddenly fractured and while everything seemed to look exactly the same, I knew everything had profoundly changed. How can you lose someone that you assumed was going to be there for the rest of your life? In the last few years, my brother and I had become a kick-ass team, organized and united in taking care of our parents. He took care of the finances, I took care of the medical, and we both found great satisfaction in being able to work so well together on this most important job—taking care of the people we loved the most.

At some level, I knew I was in shock. Even writing this now brings back that heart-racing, sweaty-palms, blurry feeling I had. The only thing that seemed to get me to move was thoughts of my mom, sister-in-law, and niece. At that point my mother was the only one who didn't know. How was I ever going to be able to tell my mother that her only son had died?

I knew instinctively that I could not tell her this news on the phone—she and I were still recovering from the loss of my father which was raw and hurting. So I bought myself a plane ticket to California so I could tell her the news in person. It was the worst plane ride of my life.

In the end, I was enormously grateful I had been able to tell her in person because at that moment, there was no one I needed more in the world than my mother and I knew there was no one she needed more than me. After we spoke, I hunkered down at our family's dining room table to check in with my sister-in-law on the West Coast. Did she want my mom and me to come and stay with them? She said thank you, but they were okay. Did they need anything? They were doing as well as could be expected. We stayed in constant contact, taking comfort from each other and reassuring each other that we were all going to be fine.

During that first week after it happened, I helped my mother with all the condolences that were flooding in from all the wonderful friends and family who wanted to call and visit and bring us so much food that we didn't know what to do with it. We never quite knew what kind of call or visit it would be. Some callers would end up sobbing on the phone, not able to control their own grief as they tried to comfort us. Some sent lovely email messages. Some came over to reminisce about how as a young boy David ran around getting in constant trouble. And some came to distract us. Probably my favorite visit that week was a cousin who came over, sat down, and immediately started showing us a truly extensive set of photos of his last two vacations. And you know what? That was the most pleasant diversion my mom and I had all week. He didn't mention my brother once—he didn't have to. We all knew what we were feeling, and it was just so incredibly refreshing to focus on pictures of enormous mugs of beer in German beer gardens and delicious plates of food in Tokyo restaurants for a change!

When I got back home to New York after seven days with my mother, my life came to a screeching halt. I went from a state of being highly anxious to severe depression. I told as few people as possible and certainly did not post anything on social media—such a public declaration would have meant it had really happened. It felt like a tsunami of deep sadness hit me just as I was getting out of the shower, naked, unawares, and totally vulnerable.

Of course I knew I was not the first person to be faced with an unexpected death, but I was shocked at how earth-shattering and devastating it actually could be. I found myself going through cycles of calm and grief with longer periods of grief occurring when I happened to come across anything that reminded me of my brother.

This was not a bright summer season.

It dawned on me that I was going to have to get through what was to be the hardest thing I had ever done in my life: writing and giving my brother's eulogy. This was even more poignant for me because just three months before, when my father passed away, as my brother and I planned my father's memorial service, I remember so clearly knowing that I could not handle speaking at his service—I was too shaken. That day, my brother had taken the lead, giving the perfect eulogy for our dad. It was heartfelt and included a story I had never heard before about my dad's undying optimistic spirit that perfectly captured his supportive, kind, and loving presence in our lives.

This time was different. I was on my own with no backup. And this event was going to be really big. My brother had a huge network of friends stretching all the way back to elementary school and we were forced to limit the guest list to two hundred friends and family, though more wanted to attend what we were calling David's "Celebration of Life." I wanted to say something that truly reflected him—his funny side, his family side, his astounding network of friends—and the sheer shock that everyone was feeling. I really didn't know if I was going to be able to write such a speech—I had never done one before. And even if I did, I didn't know if I was going to be able to actually get through it without crying incoherently in front of everyone. Talk about a fear- and anxiety-provoking situation.

The thing that ended up helping the most during that time was my regular morning tea meditations. In the month before the event as I sat in meditation each morning, I wasn't trying to write the speech. In fact, I actively tried NOT to think about writing that speech. But in the clearing of my mind that came during those meditations, I felt the space open up to reveal exactly what I wanted to say. I, of course, knew it all along. I needed to clear away the fear, anxiety, and sadness that were clouding those thoughts. I also had this thought—almost a premonition—that I needed to figure out how to not just get beyond the pain but make something meaningful out of it. I think I was, in the moment, trying to transform all these emotions from obstacles into tools. What came forward were memories about the week I had spent visiting my brother in Shanghai just the year before, and how I wished I had visited him earlier and more often. I thought about how even though we didn't get to spend a lot of time together, I realized how much I loved him, despite never saying it to him out loud. All these thoughts seemed to crystalize after the meditations, so that when I sat in front of my laptop at my dining room table to finally write the eulogy, it all flowed out of me more easily than I would ever have imagined.

On what would have been my brother's fifty-first birthday, I gave him the loving, caring, and heartfelt send-off I had wanted to give him. I felt him there with us that day. I've given hundreds, maybe even thousands of talks in my career. This was by far the most meaningful and the one I will never forget. I was nowhere near "recovered" from this terrible double loss of both my father and brother, but giving that eulogy was a first important step toward my recovery that continues today. I also realized that terrible grief and anxiety pushed me to come up with the words that reflected not just my love but my whole family's love for my brother. In part because of the depth of that grief itself, I was able to articulate everything that was so fun and great and truly unique about my brother.

Sometimes I can't believe I was able to give that eulogy given the state I was in. It was probably my life's most profound example of resilience thus far. If there was ever a time when I needed to literally pull myself together and step beyond my emotions and perform, that was it.

Looking back on this time in my life, I realize now that this was truly my own personal superpower moment. It was the moment that my deep grief, anxiety, and sorrow were superseded and triumphed over by my own resilience. Where did that resilience come from? Part of it came from my morning meditation practice. I had been building my meditation muscle to live in the moment and give myself some relief from the grief. That morning respite was so helpful. The other thing that helped me was the onset of a state of wonder. A few days after losing my brother, I became aware of a real sense of awe that I was still here. I began to feel intensely how incredibly lucky I was to be alive and able to enjoy the world and the people in it and the things that make me happy when my brother could not. The hardest thing during that time was the terrible guilt that I didn't do enough with him or for him. I wasn't a good enough sister; I didn't stay in touch enough; and I didn't appreciate all his amazing qualities until it was too late (this last one I still think about all the time). But maybe I could express all these thoughts and feelings in his eulogy—say it for the world to hear, and in that way affirm that I was going to learn from losing my only sibling. I also felt a new impetus to actively pursue ways to better appreciate the life I had, and especially the people in my world.

I know I'm not alone in my experience of loss, grief, and heartache. We all have to dig deep and make it through soul-sucking situations like this every single day. We are a resilient species, and many of us don't even know it. But I knew it then and I know it now: I didn't have to just make it through that eulogy; there was the rest of my life to deal with.

....

In the weeks and months after my brother's passing, I was actually surprised to find that I was getting on with my life. I began to research grief, discovering that it's not only marked by depression but also anxiety—the bad kind that I've been discussing since the outset of this book. I also began to understand that my resilience network was kicking in. Despite still mourning these losses, as the summer wore on, I was able to start summoning trickles of hope and optimism; to get out of bed in the morning ready to tackle my to-do list. I suddenly wanted (and needed) to see my closest friends. I wanted to return to my research and the many other projects I had left behind as well. I wanted to pick up the threads of writing this book. In fact, my anxiousness about getting behind in work, my worries about making headway on this book, and even being bothered by how sluggish I was feeling in my body—all this discomfort began to motivate me. Was it a struggle? Of course. It wasn't easy. But I also knew that my anxiety was guiding me to engage with the parts of my life that brought meaning. I pushed on and that's part of the complexity and mystery of human resilience.

I particularly remember one morning workout during this time. My trainer that day, Phoenix, was describing the profound mind-body benefit that comes from really pushing yourself physically in a demanding, sweat-inducing workout. She shared this quote with me from Ecclesiastes 1:18:

"With great pain comes great wisdom."

And that's when it hit me. Like a black-and-white picture exploding into full and vibrant color, I suddenly realized the depth of the wisdom that can come with terrible pain. I realized that the physical and emotional distress that I'd been experiencing since these tragedies hit was just like many forms of anxiety that I had experienced all my life: It was acting like a giant nudge to "move on," "get going," "you can do it." I was actually embodying what the neuroscientific research about anxiety describes: that it can motivate you to change and adapt. It was also showing me the magnitude of the event I was actually capable of moving on from.

This event gave me a crash course on the depths of my resilience, and being able to deliver that eulogy and fully engage in the recovery process was proof of it. But maybe the most salient outcome has been the new level of deep love and appreciation I have for my family, my friends, my supporters, and all the amazing opportunities I enjoy in my life. Talk about something shifting from black-and-white to Technicolor—this shift in my awareness, appreciation, and gratitude for all I hold dear in my life has simply been profound, like a giant highlighter showing me how good I have it and how much I have in my life.

My resilience not only comes from surviving the losses of my father and brother but also from adapting to and learning from any episode of anxiety in my life. That is the power of understanding the nature of both anxiety and resilience. It's the idea that we don't have to fight the pain, sorrow, and anxiety in our lives. We can use these powerful, negative feelings and transform them to become more whole, wiser, and to gain strength and do something new and creative with this newfound wisdom. Yes, I have not only transformed my relationship to anxiety; I have discovered an inner reserve, a strength that has fueled all aspects of my life. I do more, feel more, create more, and love more. I perform better and feel better. My life is better than it was before.

So, what is resilience?

It's tenacity in response to falling short of your goal.

It's courage to continue despite disappointment.

It's the belief that you can and will do better if you put in the effort or practice.

It's the confidence to believe that you matter.

It's an openness to learning and relearning.

It's the stamina to persevere.

....

I always knew resilience was going to be a big part of the foundation on which *Anxiety is Your Superpower* would be based, but experiencing these terrible losses just as I dove into writing dramatically changed the book and the role of resilience in it. Before these events, I was excited about sharing the idea that one could use the "warning signals" of anxiety for good. After these events, the idea of flipping your everyday anxiety from bad to good went from an exciting new idea to a mission. I realized I was using this approach to get through the most difficult times; these were not just useful ideas but profound life lessons everyone could use to improve their daily lives—from worrying over how long it has taken you to respond to an email from your boss to a personal tragedy.

So for all of you experiencing anxiety in your lives today, it is my greatest wish that you use the tools laid out in this book to build your own superpower of resilience to withstand any form of stress and anxiety, big or small, so that you can bounce back, take all the lessons learned and all the wisdom that comes with them, and move forward stronger, wiser, and more empowered. Just as I did.

5

Enhance Your Performance and Open the Door to Flow

You've probably heard that it takes about ten thousand hours of practice to become an expert in anything—a musical instrument, a sport, chess, cooking, or a foreign language. The research by K. Anders Ericsson on this topic has been written about many times, and it was made even more famous when Malcolm Gladwell described it in his bestselling book *Outliers*.[1] However, recently, a cohort of researchers reexamined the studies and research behind the 10K figure and said, quite dramatically, that the ten-thousand-hour rule was utter nonsense. Specifically, there is nothing particularly special about ten thousand hours, and while practice is clearly important to boost performance, other factors may play an even more important role.

What are those other factors that get us to expert levels of performance? Pure innate talent? Intelligence? Luck of the draw?

Perseverance? Hard work? Yes, it's all of that . . . and more. Age, experience, and environment all play a role. In other words, there's no one certain factor that can predict or ensure mastery or optimal performance of anything.

The Hungarian-American psychologist Mihaly Csikszentmihalyi has led the charge in this area of affective neuroscience research—first with his studies of elite-level athletes but later applying how optimal performance can be seen in many areas, including science, art, and music. Flow is a spectrum.[2] It's decidedly not an all-or-nothing experience. It's about the right blend of preparation, positive self-talk, and fluidity, and much of how it's activated relates to how we are learning how to unpack anxiety, its arousal and its challenges. But this research is also relevant to anxiety; in particular, the elements or characteristics that enable flow align with how we can channel the arousal of anxiety. Being able to calm our body, nurture an activist mindset, and use our attention all come into play. One new feature that flow calls upon is related to motivation. Flow requires that we become deeply engaged in and enjoy an activity, which is activated in part by the reward network of the brain. As we will see, anxiety can benefit this reward circuit or dampen it and therefore either enhance our performance or hinder it. Understanding the neuroscience of how anxiety (bad and good) interacts with the reward and motivation networks helps us to understand how we can use good anxiety to boost our performance and thereby have more chances to experience flow.

We can apply the neuroscience of optimal performance to anything we want to learn or relearn, any new skill or task we are curious about. The operative word here, however, is *want.* Using anxiety to optimize performance requires us to approach the task with enthusiasm and interest—not fear or reservations. In order to use our anxiety, we must befriend it. Let's look at how that can happen.

· PERFORMANCE ANXIETY ·

I think everyone would agree that anxiety makes performance level go down the drain, so to speak. So regardless of your hours, months, or years of practicing a skill—whether it's public speaking, playing the piano, playing tennis or basketball—anxiety not only undermines your performance but absolutely eliminates any chance of reaching optimal performance or flow. But what I've come to realize from my deep dive into this research is that just as we can learn how to nurture an activist mindset, use mistakes or failures as feedback, and use the arousal of anxiety to up our attention, we can also learn how to improve our performance and perhaps edge a bit more toward a flow experience.

In my own life I've had experiences where my bad anxiety got in the way of my ability to perform well under pressure. I've had other situations where I learned how to lean into the energy from my good anxiety to actually enhance my performance. It's important to understand how both of these experiences can happen. An example of the former is one I would rather forget. It was soon after I started my faculty position at NYU, and I was in charge of hosting a highly respected senior neuroscientist when she visited to give a talk to our department. This woman was brilliant, world-renowned, and I knew that she did not suffer fools gladly. I not only served as her official "host" at the university, which meant I would be responsible for organizing her meetings with faculty and students during her daylong visit, but one of my most important duties was to introduce her at the talk mentioned above. I had done my due diligence researching her career, including making a list of all her prominent awards. I was very motivated to give a top-notch intro that day. And when I stepped up to the podium to give that two-minute introduction, I was nervous. Perhaps it was because this particular scientist had always intimidated me a bit (okay, maybe a lot). Or perhaps it was because it was one of the first times as a young faculty member that I had introduced such a prominent speaker to my department. Maybe it was because I felt personally responsible for every aspect of her visit and put a lot of pressure on myself to give a clear, informative, insightful, and even memorable introduction. Note again that I'm talking about a two- to three-minute introduction. But because I had such high expectations for myself, that nervous energy I felt when I stepped up to the podium quickly spiraled into a classic case of bad anxiety.

I remember clear as day hearing my voice quaver and crack when I started to speak and thinking with horror that I sounded like an undergraduate giving their first in-class presentation, not a faculty member introducing a colleague. The worst part was that it was not just my voice that quavered; I lost the ability to read off the crib sheet I had brought with me. I ended up skipping the long list of accolades and rushed through to the end.

To this day, I still shudder when I recall this botched intro. My anxiety interfered so acutely that it not only played havoc with my body but on my brain—my memory had frozen, my mouth didn't seem to work normally, and I seemed to have lost the ability to simply read from the notes I had prepared that were right in front of me.

As we've seen time and again, the activation that underlies anxiety can go either way—take us down into the bad zone or ricochet us into the good zone, where all sorts of marvelous things can happen. This double-edged sword that is anxiety plays an important role in learning how to use it to optimize performance. Of course we are all vulnerable to performance anxiety: the nervous feelings, the sweaty palms, and the racing heart that come at important times, such as before taking a test, in advance of a job interview, as you walk onstage to give a speech, or before a sporting event or competition. Up to a certain point, it's good arousal: It gets your attention and motivates you. The nervousness is actually useful: It reminds you that you are doing something that is important to you—that you *get* to do something that means so much to you. But when the nervousness gets to be too much, when doubting thoughts begin to mount and fear seeps in, we can experience a kind of physical melting down; we are no longer able to use the arousal of anxiety.

· THE NEUROSCIENCE BEHIND OPTIMAL PERFORMANCE (AKA FLOW, BABY, FLOW) ·

So what is flow?

Csikszentmihalyi[3] and his colleagues, including Jeanne Nakamura,[4] came to identify a state of heightened engagement or immersion in an activity that you are performing at a high level and called it "flow." *Flow* is defined as a deeply engaged state where high skill/performance accompanies a seemingly relaxed, almost effortless state of mind, one of intense enjoyment and immersion. They also note that states of flow don't happen every day. Instead they are relatively rare occurrences that happen when the right combination of cognitive, physical, and emotional features almost magically align.

Studies focused on the relationship between arousal and performance have been going on for quite a while. Way back in 1908 something known as the Yerkes-Dodson Law[5] was established by researchers at Harvard who were trying to understand what motivates goal-directed behavior such as studying in order to do well on a test. They wanted to understand whether or not stress played a positive role in motivation. What they learned is that there is an optimal level of arousal and its resulting anxiety that maximizes performance (high point on the curve, see next page). But beyond a certain level of arousal, what we would call bad anxiety causes performance to plummet.

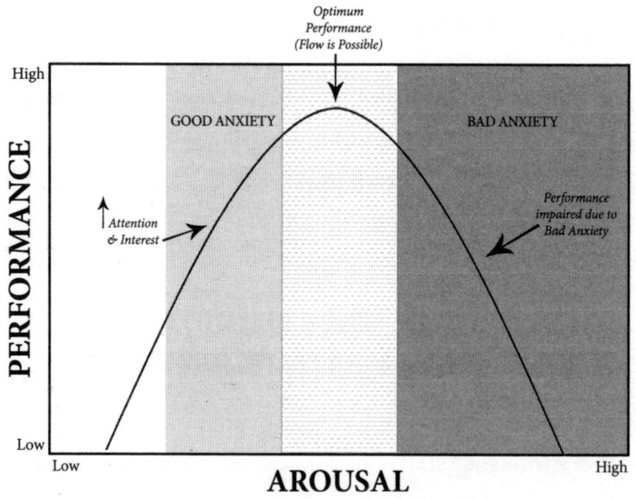

Figure 4. **Relationship Between Arousal and Performance**

This mechanism and diagram that define flow also reflect our relationship to anxiety—when we learn to channel the arousal, it's helpful, but there is a tension between the two that we need to keep in mind.

Let's spend some time looking at the left-hand side of this graph. The engagement piece implies enjoyment and pleasure. The arousal speaks to the need for some stress to provoke a state of alertness; this is the positive side of anxiety. Finally, it's the interplay of all these dimensions that prepares us or paves the way for that state of flow, where performance can be at its peak. Note that good anxiety kicks in as the arousal level starts to increase, along with an increase in focus/attention. Arousal is measured in part by peripheral measures of autonomic activity such as heart rate and skin conduction. It's also measured by cortical activity that can be detected by an EEG. Alongside this recruitment of arousal (positive energy) and attention is our interest or degree of engagement. Together these factors help make the performance take a sharp upward trajectory. It's at the very top of the performance "mountain," so to speak, when performance is optimal, that you can experience flow. This graph illustrates very well why classic flow is not experienced very often. There are a lot of elements that need to come together in order to hit the pinnacle of true "Csikszentmihalyi flow."

Another element that can predict an experience of flow is improvement. Now, of course "peak performance" is relative to any one person. My peak performance in playing the cello will always be wildly different from Yo-Yo Ma's, but the possibility of reaching my own state of flow regardless of my skill level adds to my motivation—I want to do better, I want to improve. This desire is what triggers the reward network. We remember the experience of pleasure because the brain releases dopamine, which in turn feels good. It's this good feeling that we remember and will want to repeat. The more skillful you are at something, the more efficiently your brain-body will perform. The more skillful you are, the more competent you feel. And the more competent you feel, the more relaxed you will be performing.

Looking again at the graph, it's important to note that we all walk a very fine line—you might call it walking on a razor's edge—between the point of optimal performance where flow is possible and succumbing to bad anxiety and the performance drop that comes with it. Yet another way to describe the right side of this graph where performance plummets and arousal goes sky-high is "choking." Let's take a quick look at how the science of this all-too-familiar phenomenon sheds light on how anxiety can interfere . . . or not.

· THE SCIENCE OF CHOKING ·

Sian Beilock, formerly of the University of Chicago and now president of Barnard College, has studied choking in elite-level athletes.[6] She has found that when a lot is at stake, we tend to let anxiety have its way with us. Anxiety can work against us, without many of us even realizing what's happening. Sometimes, no matter how ready we might feel, anxiety can rear its head and take over our nervous system *because we start thinking*. I'm sure in reading this you can bring to mind such a situation: You are about to take a driving test after failing twice; you are about to meet the parents of your new significant other; you are about to step into the big interview. The stakes are high and you freeze. We can all imagine our palms getting sweaty, our hearts beginning to race, and our minds racing with "what-ifs," literally cluttering the highway of our minds. It makes sense that a baseball player at bat in the ninth inning of the World Series, Tiger Woods putting on the last hole of the U.S. Open, or Michael Phelps trying to make a comeback at the Olympics might tense up and not perform to their expected ability when so much is on the line. And although their hours, months, and years of high-level training are meant to defend against choking, anxiety is a complicated player.

Beilock explains that the brain-body response to too much pressure takes up valuable "brain space" and causes maladaptive responses. The batter who gets caught up in thinking about the tilt of his wrist, the student who is trying to remember what page the formula is on, the computer programmer who wants to bring to mind a piece of code—this kind of overthinking interferes with performance and stops us from accessing skills we know we have. Does the baseball player really need to think about the wrist tilt at the bottom of the ninth? Does the student really need to think about what page the formula is on? Does the programmer really need to recall the entire code? No. If a person has practiced material or skills again and again, knows the information "by heart," then when the pressure is on, they utilize their aroused state (physiological, cognitive, and emotional) to automatically recall the information to do the task at hand: hit the ball, finish the problem, and input the code. This comes from all the hours of practice. The more we practice a certain skill or set of skills, the more our brain-body creates patterns so it can work more efficiently. And the enemy of this state of relaxation and trusting yourself is thinking.

When some kind of internal or external pressure becomes too much, the pathway to this automatic functioning gets interrupted. That's the basis of choking. When I was doing my introduction early in my career, my fear of the speaker, coupled with the pressure I was putting on myself, interfered with the preparations I had made and caused me to choke. I got caught up in the high stakes: I did not have any tools to calm my body, and I did not have the confidence to trust myself. My awareness of the situation interfered with my preparation and I left myself out to dry.

Beilock's research revealed another interesting facet of choking: It's the *perception* of stress that triggers the choking phenomenon. Beilock uncovered how even subtle stereotypes—women are worse at math than men; white men can't jump—negatively affect performance. For instance, women, if asked to check their gender before taking a test, will do more poorly. The cognitive reminder elicits an emotional response that in turn affects performance. The good news is that if asked to bring to mind their academic credentials, they will do at least 10 percent better on the test. The bottom line, again, is that cognition and emotion go hand in hand. Negative emotions can hamper our thinking and positive emotions can enhance our thinking. In terms of flow, this is why enjoyment of the activity is so essential; that pleasure is boosting our dopamine (the happy neurotransmitter), which feeds our relaxation and our performance.[7]

· TIME TO NAIL IT ·

Working with brilliant students who often put a ton of pressure on themselves, I see classic versions of choking pretty often. What makes the following story so memorable is how I watched this student ultimately tap into the power of his anxiety to optimize his performance.

Tom was really smart, articulate, and could write better than I had ever seen in a student at his level. He enjoyed writing, and it showed in his attitude and enthusiasm for the papers we wrote together. When he presented either science papers or his own data in lab meetings, he seemed in his element—funny, smart, and at ease. But put him in front of an audience full of scientists (even if he knew all of them) and he suddenly choked. He would become visibly nervous, which was even more obvious because we never saw him respond that way in lab.

After one such public meltdown where he became so overwrought that he couldn't speak, he came to me very upset and on the verge of tears. "I just don't know how to stop it—no matter how much I practice or rehearse before I do a presentation, I can't seem to handle it."

I was a bit taken aback by the sheer emotion he was expressing. Then I said, "How can I help, Tom?"

"How have you learned to be so calm during your public and academic lectures, talks, and presentations?"

"Well," I started, "I think it's because I actually like lecturing and interacting with the audience. I think my enjoyment helps me relax and pushes me to do better each time I give a talk."

In other words, wanting to improve on something that I enjoy motivates me to do my best. I can be calm during public speaking because I believe it is something that brings me pleasure—rather than believing it is something that causes me pain.

Saying this aloud gave me an insight: I had to help Tom look forward to presenting, but first he needed to build up some strategies to get him out of the fear zone so he could feel more confident. I also needed to help him stay connected to his love of writing about science; this was key to helping him relax and stay engaged.

Tom had put in time to rehearse, and he loved the science, but I realized that I had to help him figure out what could motivate him to use his anxiety. Tom had other advantages to help him get over his public speaking anxiety, such as his great sense of humor and his experience thinking on his feet wonderfully at our weekly lab meeting. So, with his permission, I decided to do a little experiment with him.

I asked him what other fears or anxieties he had beyond public speaking that he didn't mind sharing. He said he had always had anxiety about money, that the modest graduate-student stipend was not helping.

"How does this affect you?"

"I guess I've just learned to live with it. But sometimes it will keep me up at night. My student loans are still far from being paid off and I worry about finding a well-paying job in academia after graduate school."

I asked, "Can you imagine being able to live with that discomfort?"

"I guess so," he said. "I mean, I really want this degree despite the low pay I'm getting now. I love learning the science."

I then suggested that he had become used to dealing with a kind of low-grade level of discomfort in his life. He agreed.

I then asked if he realized that he could apply his strategies for managing his anxiety about money to his fear of public speaking.

He didn't think so but was willing to give it a shot.

I explained that I thought he might be able to use his tolerance for "money anxiety" to quiet his fear of public speaking. Anxieties—even when the triggers are different—are a very similar kind of activation with similar physiological responses (they activate the same stress response system and in essentially the same way). The question was, how could Tom get his public speaking anxiety tolerance up to the level of his financial anxiety tolerance? Step one was to become aware of the fact that he already managed his anxiety around money; this awareness of his stress tolerance was crucial to being able to apply it to other aspects of his life. This awareness also enabled him to shift to an activist mindset wherein he could believe he was able to bring his public speaking anxiety down to tolerable levels.

That was just step one.

Then I helped him make a strategic plan in anticipation of his third-year talk, which was coming up in the department that was required of all graduate students and Tom was already losing sleep over it.

Here is what we did:

- Together, we *practiced* his talk so that he knew everything he wanted to say and had responses for (almost) every possible probing question. I wasn't asking him to memorize his talk. In fact, it was important that he feel comfortable sharing the ideas a little differently every time so that he remained in touch with his conversational side. I wanted him to keep understanding his ideas and connections to his ideas. This rehearsal moved his understanding from working memory to more declarative memory. I asked him the hardest questions I could think of and I saw him getting better and better. As we worked, he became more and more confident and fluid, even enjoying responding to the questions in our practice sessions. A critical part of the rehearsal was my asking him the hardest and widest-ranging questions I could, as a lot of his anxiety seemed to center around fear that tended to freeze him in the face of curveballs. We both knew that despite the fact that he might give a great talk, if he didn't answer the questions with confidence, people would leave with a negative impression of his presentation. I knew from experience that a seasoned speaker starts to know the common questions that get asked and how to answer them. Yes, there will be occasional unexpected questions, but most have a particular theme that you can practice answering and get comfortable with. Also, you begin to realize that the best questions you get are the ones that bring you wonderful new insights into possible interpretations that you can think about and discuss with the audience member, which is one of the most fascinating parts of giving a talk. As I went through all my questions, I saw Tom getting better and better at answering them succinctly. I saw his confidence start to kick in and the anxiety in his face start to dissipate.

- I worked with Tom on reframing how he thought about public speaking. I reminded him that part of what he was doing in his talk was *sharing* his work and his love of science with the rest of the community. He needed to realize that his talk should reflect the enjoyment and curiosity I saw in him every day in the lab. He needed to draw on that enjoyment so he could internalize his love of the actual material.
- I gave him positive feedback, both in how hard he was working to prepare and how good the work he was presenting really was. I reiterated how proud I was of him for working so hard on this presentation and assured him that I had no doubt (which I did not) that he would do a bang-up job.

And guess what: He nailed his third-year talk! He was nervous at the beginning, but he recognized it. Rather than let his nervousness kick off a tailspin of bad anxiety, he was able to lean into all the rehearsing we'd done together and channel his good anxiety. Soon he found his rhythm and did a fantastic job. The questions were tough, and he struggled to answer some of them, but he made it through. I could see he was relieved but also very proud as his fellow graduate students came up to praise him on a job well done.

Tom upped his performance significantly but didn't quite get into flow. He loved the experience and became both excited and motivated about getting more practice to make it to flow. He was well on his way!

My bigger point in sharing Tom's story is this: Like many ambitious people, Tom was motivated to learn to manage his anxiety. He also understood that his anxiety could be helpful and productive, and bettering his performance appealed to his desire to improve. I have witnessed this pattern many times over the years with both undergraduate and graduate students. They know the material just fine—clearly at a strong A level—but they get so stressed and nervous for the exam (either written or oral) that they are not able to express that knowledge clearly on the test. They misread questions and make unnecessary errors in just following directions and end up receiving a grade that does not reflect the true state of their knowledge. What's crucial, from my point of view as a teacher, is that students learn to manage their anxiety. As we know, stress in life is inevitable; a student who opts for less stress is only hurting his or her chances of learning how to operate well under stress.

I have found that when I have the opportunity to offer feedback to a student and confirm their understanding of a topic, they feel encouraged, are less anxious, and often do better on exams (i.e., performance). This kind of positive feedback is the essence of the good old-fashioned pep talk, but it focuses on their ability to expand their stress tolerance and find a way to comfortably manage pressure.

I also encourage students to be their own best "executive coaches" for exams, especially ones that are worth a large percentage of their grade. I suggest that they treat taking an exam like training for a sporting event—practice, rehearse, and give yourself a pep talk. What does this look like? After going over the material and answering any practice questions provided or, better yet, making up your own to determine if you understand the material fully, tell yourself that you have GOT this! Go over in your mind all the quality time you've spent reviewing the material and visualize yourself methodically and calmly answering all the questions the professor throws at you one by one with no problem. If you get stuck, simply move on to all the material you DO know and come back to the problem question later. Then on the day of the exam, say out loud to yourself, "I am going to CRUSH this exam! I studied hard and know the material like a CHAMP!"

Positive self-talk goes hand in hand with visualization. Why does visualization help? Because it allows you to believe in the ultimate antianxiety scenario. Visualization allows you to create a new model in your head for how you will approach a potentially anxiety-provoking situation and provide another path for yourself. If you have always had a lot of anxiety around particular exams, maybe start with visualizing yourself taking the exam and clearly and calmly writing down all of your well-thought-out answers. See yourself in the situation as you want to show up. You can build on the simple image of yourself in the exam by adding details about how the pen will feel in your hand or the sense of calm that you will experience during the exam. Visualizations can be very powerful but they take practice and a fair bit of imagination. Keep focused on positive outcomes that relate to the anxiety-producing situation.

Like any new habit you want to form, start small and build from there.

· CAN YOU LEARN TO FLOW? ·

Flow relies on your ability to calm your anxiety, flip it, and then use it. And though elite-level flow experienced by masters like Yo-Yo Ma and Michael Phelps may seem out of reach, we all can get a taste of flow and aspire to it. Anytime you're approaching that zone it feels amazing—almost like a drug. You lose track of time, you are completely caught in the moment, enjoying yourself, and all cylinders are on go. Flow not only requires joy but generates it and enhances performance to an even higher level that will tend to generate even more flow states. Who wouldn't want more flow in their lives?

So what if we redefine flow? For example, instead of the ten thousand hours of work to get to the ultra-high performance level required for classic Csikszentmihalyi flow, what if we consider for a moment something I will call *micro flow*. Let me explain. Micro flow is a flow state that may be shorter in duration than the classic Csikszentmihalyi flow but is more frequent and can be used to enrich our lives as well as our performance in a significant way. In a sense micro flow is simply giving yourself an opportunity to enjoy yourself. Micro flow gets at the heart of the neuroscience: Any experience can become flowlike if it incorporates intention, engagement, and fun. When we experience this kind of mind-body pleasure, our brains release dopamine and we store that memory and use it to motivate us in the future.

Consider some examples of micro flow moments:

- a deep savasana at the end of a hard yoga class
- a deep and refreshing night's sleep after a really hard week

- an uplifting and/or hilarious conversation with your best friend
- the deep state of relaxation you achieve after an amazing massage
- a super-efficient day where you got five things done (and it only took fifteen minutes)
- a fantastic neighborhood effort to rescue a cat from a tree where everyone had a shared goal and felt truly in tune with one another

None of these examples may be profound Csikszentmihalyi flow—that's clear. Yet all of them include relaxation and enjoyment after an exertion of hard work or deep engagement, and therefore they produce a reward. Like classic Csikszentmihalyi flow, micro flow has a strong motivational component. What is this good for? These more frequent moments of flow serve not only to decrease bad anxiety and enhance good anxiety but also to help you take full advantage of the joyful moments in your everyday life, and that will be one of the most effective rest, recovery, and motivational strategies you have.

· GO FOR IT! ·

Not long ago I was invited by a Russian business group to present at their big annual conference in Moscow. I was standing backstage at the Olympic Stadium preparing to address a crowd of thousands about the topic of my first book, the transformative effects of exercise on the brain. The setup was grand, and as I looked from the wings out across the stage and into the enormous stadium, I could feel myself begin to get nervous because I suddenly realized this was probably the biggest audience I had ever spoken to in my life. I remember my sweaty palms and my heart thumping so loud that I wondered if the tech people hovering around me could hear it. Just the day before I had seen two of the other speakers on this program, Malcom Gladwell (of ten thousand hours fame!) and Richard Gere (of *Pretty Woman* fame), walk out onto this stage and give stellar presentations. Could I do the same?

To increase my anxiety even more, when I had sat in the audience the day before to listen to Gere and Gladwell, I realized that they welcomed all speakers onto the stage with fireworks that went off at the front of the stage. I was so glad I saw the fireworks the day before or they would have really freaked me out—obviously, most stages do not come with their own fireworks display! I stood backstage, thinking about the magnitude of the moment and preparing for those fireworks that would go off when I stepped onto the stage. Now, that might have pushed me over the edge into stress and bad anxiety and back to my "introduction of the speaker" nightmare scenario of years before. But this time was very different. I knew my talk cold, and not only that—I loved giving it. I remember thinking clearly, with a kind of hyper-precise awareness, at that moment right before I stepped onto the stage, *I'm going to give them a talk worthy of those fireworks that are about to go off for me!*

And I did.

I used my prefrontal cortex to refocus on the joy of conveying a message I really believed in and away from the fear of failure or worry that I would not be "as good as." Instead of freaking me out, those fireworks actually inspired me to amp up my energy and enthusiasm level and therefore my talk level. Was I nervous beforehand? Of course! But those nervous feelings were being put to use as motivation to rise to the occasion and nail my presentation to match them—my good anxiety in action! And the best part was that despite the size of the venue and the fact that most of the audience was listening to me through headphones with a Russian translator, I could feel the audience completely engaged through the whole talk!

It's true that I have not felt "Csikszentmihalyian" very many times in my life. But I felt it on that stage in Moscow. Maybe it was because of the energetic boost I got from those fireworks, or maybe it was because when I got to a key line in my talk that came just two minutes in, where I say, "Exercisc is the most transformative thing that you can do for your brain today," the audience actually started applauding—something that had NEVER happened before! Maybe it was because I had a Russian drummer who came onstage twice to provide the music for two mini exercise sessions that I invited everyone to participate in and they all did. It was one of the most memorable talks I have ever given not just for the unique venue but because of the participation of that wonderful audience. I felt like the audience and I found flow together during that talk.

6

Nurture an Activist Mindset

Right before my fortieth birthday, I hit an emotional brick wall. I had spent the previous twenty years studying, researching, and pushing myself academically and then professionally. I was a driven achiever and really had little identity beyond that. The girl who grew up loving Broadway shows? Gone. The young woman who traveled to France, became smitten with the language, culture, food, and wine? Gone. The young woman who fell madly in love with a young French musician? Gone. At forty, after spending all of my adult life in academia, I suddenly began to feel like I was just a head on a stick.

I worked obsessively. I gave myself no time to rest, relax, and recharge. I didn't like how I looked or how I felt. I was cut off from people, communicating only with a small circle of people that included a few friends who did not live in New York City. At this time, I was not close to either my parents or my brother. I was a bundle of nerves—anxious, worried, and running on fumes. This was what in part drove me to work so hard: Productivity and success at work was one of my few pleasures in life. My other pleasure was food, which had led to my twenty-five-pound weight gain. What made this situation worse was my putting on a "happy, energetic face" for the outside world. I didn't want to be seen as a lonely person with no friends. I wanted to be seen as energetic, happy, and active. But projecting this happy face to the outside ended up making me more anxious and lonely than if I had shown my true feelings.

At first, I had no idea how to get myself out of this situation. I felt like I was pushing a three-ton elephant up a mountain. But then, as I very consciously shifted gears, relying on my understanding of science and a desperate need for change, I began to make a few small adjustments. I figured that if I felt better in my body, I might feel better in my head. So I changed my diet, stopped eating out so often at my much-beloved NYC restaurants, and cleaned up my meals. Next, I committed to exercising more regularly. It took some time to discover a form of exercise I actually enjoyed and thank heavens I live in New York where there's a crazy abundance of options. Ultimately, I tried and loved a class called intenSati, which is a blend of yoga, dance, and aerobics combined with positive spoken affirmations. I became obsessed. The final new thing I added to my life was meditation. This, too, took time to integrate into my daily life. I cannot say that overnight I established a regular meditation practice. But as I tried apps, classes, and doing simple sequences on my own, I gradually learned how to meditate—indeed, it's all about learning what works for you. There is no one way to meditate; there is no right or wrong.

I paid close attention to how I responded to these new stimuli and tracked my results. I was creating and collecting my own data in real time. What I observed was nothing short of transformational: Yes, I lost unwanted extra weight. Yes, I began to feel more energetic and positive about my body. Yes, I felt calmer and more focused. I was able to sleep better, find time to relax, and not work *all* the time. But the most significant transformation I was experiencing in real time was a profound shift in my mood and attitude toward myself and my life.

As I took a step back and tried to understand and analyze these changes in my life as if they were being made by someone else, some questions occurred to me: What enables one person to learn and grow from even the most challenging experiences in their life, while another is beaten down by them? What drives another person to take a deeply painful situation and dig their way out of it, not to simply survive but thrive? What drove *me* to move beyond my very real feelings of missing out on life and try to do something about it? What drove me to flip the situation, not necessarily knowing what would result?

I have always counted myself lucky to have been born with a natural curiosity about the world (which explains my chosen profession as professor and researcher). In fact, in science, we use failure almost as a litmus test in experiments. In his article "A Celebration of Failure,"[1] Joseph Loscalzo, physician and professor of medical education at Harvard Medical School, points out, "Failure is, of course, part of the scientific method. All well designed experiments are framed in terms of the null hypothesis, which more often turns out to hold rather than its alternate." This familiarity with failure was not new to me—I just had never personalized it. Indeed, in this heap of anxiety, I was forced to see my situation as a kind of failure, but one that I could surely learn to understand.

Science says that it's possible to nurture this kind of productive reaction toward failures, mistakes, or even what we might call bad luck. We are born with an ability to use literally anything that happens to us (both good and bad) as an opportunity to learn, grow, and expand our horizons; that same capacity can also lead us to interpret anything that happens to us (both good and bad) as problematic, frightening, and unreliable. This lens through which we interpret and process our experience and, most important, our belief in our own competence is called *mindset*. This fascinating and hot research topic is rooted in the work of Carol Dweck,[2] a Stanford psychologist and educator who through years of research identified that children, students, and adults demonstrate one of two mindsets—one that is fixed or one that is growth-oriented.

Dweck was interested in understanding why some students persist in spite of failure or obstacles while others give up. She focused her research on how students perceive their competence or intelligence. She discovered that young people, for instance, who believe that intelligence is already determined developed a fixed mindset and will therefore have a harder time persevering. They also tend to believe that any mistake or failure is a demonstration (proof) of their limited intelligence or competence.

On the other hand, young people who believe that intelligence can be learned and grown with effort tend to treat mistakes as information that can lead to better solutions next time, demonstrating a growth mindset. Young people—and adults it turns out—who are growth-oriented see themselves as continually learning, able to improve themselves and their circumstances. The good news is that Dweck has demonstrated that it's possible to develop a growth mindset. In general, she identifies this process as having four specific steps:

- First, you have to learn how to hear the "voice" of the fixed mindset, that voice that says there is a limit to what you can achieve in any situation.
- Second, you have to consciously recognize that you have a choice: to listen to this limiting belief in your own power or listen to a growth mindset voice, one that says you have control over your own stress response.

- Third, you will then need to actively talk back to the negative, self-limiting voice with a positive, growth-oriented voice. This may seem hokey but it's a form of rehearsal and practice. Instead of "I'll never get through this situation. I just can't take it anymore. Forget it. I just suck," try "This is a pretty stressful situation, but I know it will pass. I can do x, y, or z, which I know will make me feel better and more grounded. Then I can figure out next steps."
- Finally, take action. This means figuring out what to do. This is when you walk the talk and act on the knowledge that a mistake, obstacle, or negative feedback is information that informs your thoughts and actions.

I have witnessed many students over the years go from a fixed mindset to one that is growth-oriented. Not only do they become more engaged, motivated students, they often improve their overall academic performance. But what is even more relevant to us and anxiety is how this shift in mindset opens the door to what I call the "flip."

When you pay attention to the initial responses to stress, as anxiety begins to make itself known, you have a choice: You can let it have its way or you can make a choice and take action and respond in a different way to stress. This is your first step in taming anxiety and learning how to channel it.

An important part of being able to "flip" one's experience of anxiety from all negative to something neutral or even positive relies on a conscious decision to do so. I refer to this conscious choice as an *activist mindset,* and it's tied to the very nature of the brain's plasticity: It is an active choice to use anxiety as a catalyst for change, a way to reframe anxiety from being a problem to being a lesson. When you develop an activist mindset (think of it as a purposeful-growth mindset), you become able to assert more top-down control of your attitude and orientation toward the bad, uncomfortable feelings associated with anxiety, shifting both your experience of the bad feelings (i.e., they tend to lessen) *and* your belief that you can channel them in positive ways.

You know that aphorism "What doesn't kill you makes you stronger"? That points to a crucial aspect of an activist mindset: learning to trust that anxiety won't kill you and knowing how to focus your strength to get through. This way of thinking enables you to handle a situation, event, or experience despite its discomfort, learn from it, and then apply that new learning in a productive, generative direction. The full power of an activist mindset involves becoming more aware of how your attitudes toward yourself shape the way you interpret or appraise the events or situations in your life. When it feels like a door has slammed on you, anxiety can lead you to feel like there's no way out of the room; the activist mindset allows you to take a step back and look for a window.

When I was in the midst of my life crisis, my constant high level of worry kept me focused on only the negative possibilities on the horizon: What if I didn't get tenure? What if I was unceremoniously kicked out of my faculty position? What if I was never able to lose those twenty-five extra pounds I had gained? What if nobody ever cared if I lost those twenty-five pounds?

In order to do anything to actually change my situation, I first had to acknowledge just how bad I felt. After months and probably years of just trying to push through the discomfort or making myself work even harder to avoid the bad feelings, I had to actually admit to myself that something was wrong. Stopping and allowing myself to feel the feelings meant that I could not simply short-circuit those worry sessions; I had to actually face my feelings and decide whether I wanted to live inside them or try to move through. I realized that I needed to find a positive distraction from my feelings to give myself a break from them. And I learned that when I sought out workout classes that were complicated enough, I would be so focused on the exercise that I didn't have a chance to think about anything else. I learned that it is impossible to worry about your job security if you are in the middle of a kickboxing class that requires every ounce of your brain-body power to follow along with the complex choreography.

So in that way, I pushed past some of those negative feelings and was able to give myself a much-needed break. But when I look back, I realize that even then I was still avoiding something really important. My anxiety was a big red flashing sign that was really saying, *You need more social interaction and friends and friendship and love in your life! You are not a robot that only works! Pay attention to all these negative emotions I'm sending you; they are giving you a message! These negative emotions are VALUABLE!*

I had to acknowledge that I had a choice: to keep doing what I was doing or make an adjustment. That point came when I realized and, more important, admitted that I was not very happy in my life. Part of this realization was that checking off all the academic boxes on the way to tenure and getting a "seat at the academic table" in terms of publication and speaking invitations would not a happy life make. I also had to face the fact that though I was living in New York—my lifelong dream city—which was full of opportunities to enjoy myself (Amazing restaurants! Broadway! Museums galore!), I was doing this enjoying mostly by myself. This realization made me take a deep look at my life and think about not just what I was doing that was adding to my anxiety but what I wasn't doing, what I was missing. Vacation. Travel. Friends. My love of languages. At the time, my attitude toward vacation was "Because I'm currently single, I won't be able to experience any real FUN vacations all on my own so no need to plan anything special." This attitude, combined with keeping my head down and working hard, was the best way to avoid feeling bad, leaving me chained to my lab bench in what was an unhealthy way. However, the positive feedback I was getting from changes I was making elsewhere in my life gave me the space to consider my options. I set out to explicitly shift my attitude toward vacations to "Because I am not attached, I have the luxury of going wherever my heart desires with no one else's schedule or preferences to limit me. What a treat!"

So what did I do? I decided to go on the most extraordinary vacation I could think of. And I had the perfect idea. I had gone on a weekend spa vacation, where one of the fitness instructors had told me about an adventure travel company he worked for. The organization brought people from all over the world to the most beautiful locations, where they got to travel and experience new cultures at the same time. I thought, *That's it! I'm going to break out of my rut by going on a spectacular adventure travel vacation.* My first trip was to Greece to go ocean kayaking with a group of wonderful guides and about fifteen hardy adventure travelers (including one solo traveler—me!). We kayaked from one little Greek seaside town to another, enjoying all the fresh delicious food, getting lots of exercise, and even touring Greek ruins. It was a spectacular trip! What a treat to meet all the other modern-day explorers in a location so different from New York City. That trip began a run of adventure travel that included touring Victoria Falls and the Zambezi River on the border of Zambia and Zimbabwe, rafting the Cotahuasi River in Peru, and traveling all through China.

I remember the freedom and joy that changed the summer months from just more of the same unending work to my time for an exciting new life adventure. This was just the first shift in a long line of mindset shifts I experienced after I took control of my initial anxiety levels. As I began to tease out the power of this shift in attitude (I didn't call it an activist mindset until later), I started to play a game with myself: Would I be able to shift my anxiety about money?

I began by examining any beliefs that were holding me back from making true changes. If you believe that unicorns are real and have magical powers, then you will live your life with that belief system in place. If you believe that the number of hours you work corresponds to how productive a person you are, then you live your life that way and spend many hours at work. For example, my lifelong fear of lack of money (anyone else with me on this one?) is founded on my fear-based belief that money is hard to come by, that it's hard to find new sources of it, and that it is always scarce. What if I gave myself permission to identify evidence of the fact that 1) I make a good salary that meets my needs; and 2) I've never not been able to pay my bills or take a vacation when I planned ahead for it? By consciously reminding myself of these realities, I give myself the opportunity to update the beliefs that are fueling my anxiety. When I decided to found a technology startup based on my research, I immediately ran right up against my beliefs about money scarcity. About a year in, it became clear how expensive starting a new company would be; I would have to put in a whole lot more of my own money and savings than I ever thought I would. Instead of giving up or letting my anxiety about money stop me from persisting, I decided to actively reframe, reshape, and even resculpt my beliefs about money.

My new attitude toward money now looks something like this: "I am great at finding new sources of money and always have options just around the corner. I know I have to spend money (wisely) to get products and more money to come in, so I happily spend money to get the job done. There is plenty of money for a good idea and I believe in my idea and I believe there will be the funding out there to back it."

Here's how my attitude shifted:

Table 2.

Old Mindset	New Activist Mindset
Money is scarce	Money is plentiful
I'm in it alone	I have a huge network of people who support me
I need to make everyone else happy	Focusing on achieving my life's goal is the best way forward
I am a person with a small number of very good friends	I have an abundance of wonderful friends
Only if you work constantly will you succeed in life	Joy, laughter, and fun is the best way to recharge your brain so it can fire on all cylinders
I'm ashamed of my failures	I learn and grow from each and every failure in my life

I needed to find a way to shift from being too afraid to risk money to being afraid of the risks, but also believing they were worth taking because I had reliable resources and access to capital.

Realizing that I had the power to calm my anxiety about money was a game changer for me. I felt an incredible sense of relief and control. I was able to identify beliefs that were clouding my ability to accurately assess a situation, and then shift those beliefs to ones that could serve me. Each time I did it, it was like my world expanded. That is not to say that I can snap my fingers and suddenly create all this money in my life—of course it's not that simple! But what I was able to do was dismantle the walls that were blocking me from even trying to reach toward the goals I wanted to reach for. Nurturing an activist mindset takes thought, commitment, and continued awareness of and willingness to tolerate discomfort. It's not that my anxiety about money has disappeared, but I keep trying and reap the benefits when I do.

As I was able to calm my bad anxiety and start to more actively cultivate an activist mindset, I also came to understand the "real" function of my anxiety: It was a warning system. My anxiety was triggered when my life started to approach the boundaries of my limiting beliefs—when I took risks, dreamed big, dared to step outside my comfort zone. When I held my anxiety at arm's length to consider it for what it was, I saw that it looked like outdated and unhelpful beliefs: The fear/anxiety I had about how expensive it was to launch a new startup was born from the fact that I believed money was always a scarce commodity. The anxiety and nerves I felt about planning a true vacation for myself stemmed from my avoidance of all the negative feelings. My anxiety was a sign that my plans and belief systems were out of sync.

The warning system of anxiety never goes away, but I started to see how I could use it to my advantage.

· JARED: JOLTING OUT OF BAD ANXIETY AND INTO A NEW ACTIVIST MINDSET ·

Remember how Jared was stuck living at home two years after college, immobilized by his anxiety and depression? His first step out of anxiety paralysis was when his parents gave him an ultimatum that he either get a job or move out. They also reminded him that he had choices, options. That he was capable of holding down a job, even if it wasn't the one he'd dreamed of while in college.

His parents' push jolted something deep inside Jared: He got mad. First, he was angry at his parents with an "I'll show them" attitude. But then, as he searched online for jobs, he got even angrier. He was smart, he was resourceful. Was he stuck? Yes. But was he capable of figuring out something to do? Yes.

His parents' demand also forced him to acknowledge just how ashamed he'd been feeling about not having a job and not having any direction. But this time, rather than sink into the shameful feelings, he held on to his anger as if it were a life raft. And it kind of was.

Jared remembered that his mother had mentioned in passing a volunteer service program in Costa Rica, where volunteers were trained to build housing and teach English at the same time. It was a yearlong commitment and Jared had minored in Spanish. He quickly researched the program, filled out an online application, and was accepted. It seemed like a good fit. Though he felt terrified and very anxious, he also felt like the job was something he could do, so he pushed himself out the door and onto the plane. He felt alone and desperate, but those feelings were not as large as the shame he was feeling stuck living in his parents' basement.

Almost as soon as Jared stepped off the plane in the capital of San José and met some of his work compatriots from the program, he started to feel himself coming back to life. The dark, moody feelings that had been like a cold, wet blanket encasing him began to lift. Over the next six months, Jared began to adjust. His anxiety and depression did not disappear, but in this new setting, he was gradually building his tolerance of his own discomfort. He became engrossed in the families, the culture, the village. His work was physically demanding—he was part of a small team that literally helped build homes in a remote village in the hills in the middle of the Northern Zone of Costa Rica. But the job demanded two things that Jared desperately needed: physical exertion that woke up his body and redirection of his attention off himself and his job/housing/life predicaments and onto others.

As he became more physically active (it was a ten-hour hike just to get to the remote village where he would be working), he could feel his high school and college level of energy return, his mood lift, and a sense that his life was not all bad. And most importantly, he was not feeling as anxious about everything. He also benefited from the increased social interaction required by this job. His job required that he speak to the kids (he was teaching English, after all) and communicate with his colleagues as they spent their spare time building housing structures for the community. This social interaction gave him positive feedback: He was valued, his work was meaningful. And with this feedback he was able to consciously reevaluate his own worthiness.

Jared did a 180-degree transformation: Being thrown into purposeful physical, emotional, cognitive, and social activity not only gave him new meaning and purpose but allowed him to make a very conscious shift in his mindset. He had a strong memory from when he was still living with his parents of his fear that he wouldn't find anything meaningful to do with his life, his anxiety over the mounting pressure that his parents were putting on him to move out, and his bad anxiety–fueled hopelessness. He was now able to use his negative emotions to help his transformation. By contrast, in Costa Rica he had an exciting, new, and totally inspired purpose. Instead of seeing a future trapped in his parents' basement, he could see a career in teaching or with charity organizations or a combination of the two opening up before his eyes. Instead of having no clue which direction his career might take after college, he knew he would be an excellent and caring teacher. Instead of feeling isolated with no close friends for support, he could feel that in this community of caring and socially minded teachers, he had found his tribe. Because he had made such a dramatic and almost instantaneous change in his life, Jared was able to see how with the lessening of his bad anxiety he was able to really apply a new mindset (in truth, it usually takes more time) toward himself and his life. And it showed on his face, in his attitude, in his personal and professional relationships, and in his new relationship with himself. It was a beautiful thing to see.

So what new circuits were being activated in Jared's brain? What was behind the jolt out of bad anxiety and the resulting shift in mindset?

From a neuroscience perspective, we know a lot about the brain circuits activated in anxiety.[3] Before Jared got to Costa Rica, there was likely a strong activation of the amygdala that was amplified by a key part of the frontal lobe, called the dorsal anterior cingulate cortex, among other interconnected brain areas associated with the feelings of anxiety and depression. After Jared was welcomed by his new community in Costa Rica, his amygdala, dorsal anterior cingulate cortex, and the ventromedial prefrontal cortex would have begun to calm down. The dramatic change of scenery for Jared literally changed his brain activations for the better. The negative triggers of his old environment were removed, and the new and positive stimuli were able to wake up his nervous system. The change in his environment acted as a new, positive stressor that lessened his bad anxiety and also prompted a new awareness of his own emotional state.

We'd also see that his prefrontal cortex and anterior cingulate cortex would be more active and that in general there was a lot more interactivity between the regions of the brain. It was as if the positive emotions acted like lubrication on a rusty engine, bringing Jared back to life.

In Jared's case, he found a fast track to flip his anxiety because:

1) His physical activity amped up, and the movement allowed him to excise some of the stress chemicals that had been stuck in his body.

2) He transported himself to a completely new environment that no longer contained any of his old and well-established anxiety triggers, so he was able to create new responses.

3) He revved up his social stimulation, which made him feel more connected to others, which in turn released oxytocin, a hormone that made him feel happier.

4) He was suddenly engaged in activities that made him feel valuable, shifting his perspective about his life's purpose and his ability to contribute to the world.

Moreover, Jared became *aware* that these adjustments were helping him change his life in a profound way. Because this shift happened so quickly, he could literally compare the limiting beliefs that had been going through his mind nonstop before his move to Costa Rica ("I will never find a job. I will never have anywhere to live that is nicer than my parents' basement. I am all alone in this. I have no idea what I want to do with my life") to a shockingly different activist mindset that had him declaring that he had found direction in his life, he had found the tribe he wanted to be part of, and he had the natural talent and energy to make this into an exciting career. He actually recognized his shiny new belief system from happier days in high school and college. He just needed a way to shift out of the bad anxiety that had taken hold (and to find this program in Costa Rica) to allow him to find that side of himself again that knew how to use an activist mindset to work through insecurities and indecision.

I'm not saying that Jared will not stumble or will live a life without doubts, fears, or anxiety for the rest of his days; more than likely, Jared is oriented a bit toward the anxious side—and that is absolutely fine. But by listening to what his anxiety was telling him was off, he was able to propel himself into a novel situation that alleviated the source of anxiety—his insecurities, self-doubt, and fear that he didn't know what to do. Physically removing himself from the site of his anxiety kickstarted his learning how to channel his anxiety and enabled him to change, and his awareness of this change is part of what constitutes his activist mindset.

· REAPPRAISING OUR ATTITUDES ·

A growth mindset utilizes the act of reappraisal we discussed in Part One. When you reappraise a situation, you exercise what neuroscientists call *cognitive flexibility*—viewing the same situation in a different light. This flexibility can be the difference between feeling trapped in a situation without escape and being able to find creative solutions to resolve a problem. For many, anxiety can come from the feeling of inevitability surrounding a certain outcome, feeling as though there's no way to solve a problem, undo an embarrassment, or avoid a bad situation. Reappraisal is a powerful tool to use in specific situations to allow you to start to break down your anxiety triggers one by one and deal with them in a different way. Reappraisal can help you see a situation in a different way, much like a coat of paint can transform the atmosphere in a familiar room. In this case, adopting an activist mindset asks that you practice thinking about negative emotions like anxiety as information—this choice teaches us to "see" our feelings instead of simply succumb to them. When I made that first observation that I was stuck in bad anxiety, that I was up against that brick wall, I became aware that there was a difference between how I felt and what was accurate. It was just enough mental room for me to shift into scientist mode and begin to look at my feelings as separate from myself. This is the beginning of adopting an activist mindset, and of flipping anxiety from bad to good.

Using an activist mindset to reappraise your situation can actually be the start of shifting your attitude about the situation into something that is actually productive. Recent neuroscience research that dives deeper into the brain basis of attitude and evaluation helps shed light on this fascinating topic. For example, one study from Stanford[4] showed that more positive attitudes about math performance in school-age children were not only associated with better math performance but also with higher levels of activity in the hippocampus when solving math problems. In other words, having a positive, can-do attitude makes us more functional—emotionally and cognitively. On the flip side, a number of other studies show that depression, anxiety, and overall negative attitudes lead to poorer performance. While correlation does not necessarily mean causation, one possible interpretation is that the positive math attitudes contributed to the better math performance (and stronger hippocampal activation).

Key studies by William Cunningham[5] and his colleagues suggest that we have the capacity to shift and change our attitudes, which is exactly what the activist mindset calls on us to do as a way to help us change our evaluations. Cunningham calls this an iterative reprocessing (IR) framework. This is a fancy way of saying that in a complex world we are always using new information to reevaluate and/or change our attitudes about particular topics. For example, is Lance Armstrong a hero for surviving cancer and giving both hope and lots of money to help support other cancer survivors like himself or is he villain number one of the doping world? These appraisals are modulated based on current information and the framework we are using for evaluation (e.g., cancer vs. doping). Our attitudes are processed by a network of areas centered in the orbitofrontal cortex, and they have the capacity to be modulated by information processed and evaluated in the lateral prefrontal cortex. These attitudes can have a positive or negative effect on our behavior, and it is completely within our power to decide which effect they have.

· THE POWER OF THE NEGATIVE CONTRAST EFFECT ·

The negative contrast effect, first noted by Leo Crespi in 1942,[6] is a phenomenon that psychologists use to describe the way something can seem more appealing when it's compared to something significantly less appealing. Here's a simple example of how a negative contrast effect can play out in real life, mine in particular. This experience took place when I was giving my first-ever "real" science talk as a graduate student at a prestigious learning and memory conference at UC Irvine. I had practiced hours upon hours, making sure that I knew my talk by heart; nonetheless, I was still very nervous. My palms were sweaty and I could feel my heart racing. My mind was filled with a whirlwind of thoughts about stumbling up onstage and forgetting my lines. The student who went before me (in this session, only students were presenting) had clearly not practiced his talk. The poor guy was not fluent in the information on his slides and fumbled through the whole thing; everyone, including me, just could not wait until he finished so as to end his (and our) misery. But watching him fumble also made me realize that I was a lot more prepared than I was giving myself credit for; I *had* reviewed my slides over and over; I *had* practiced what I was going to say. I realized that the bar for success was set a little lower than I had been imagining. I went next. Compared to the poor guy's talk, mine seemed like the highlight of the day. I got loads of positive feedback for that very first science talk I gave. The experience even began to establish a new mindset for me about public speaking: "I am an excellent public speaker."

This is what negative contrast can do: help you feel like things are actually much better than they could be and allow you to start seeing the bright side in almost any situation. Instead of only looking at the best-case scenario and worrying that you'll never achieve that, negative contrast allows you to imagine the worst-case scenario and realize how much better off you already are. Yes, it was incredibly important that I had spent the time and energy that I had ensuring I was well prepared, but that negative contrast (with the other guy providing the example) combined with the positive feedback I got cemented a strong positive belief in my public speaking abilities that has lasted to this day. You might think of it as related to "worst-case-scenario" training: With a new appraisal, a situation that seemed really bad becomes tolerable because it's not the worst-possible scenario.

....

Jared also benefited from a striking negative contrast effect. Because of the night-and-day-like difference between his environments (i.e., Mom's basement vs. remote village in Costa Rica), Jared was easily able to bring to mind how awful he'd been feeling when he was still living in his parents' basement compared to how much better he was feeling now. The uneasiness, the edginess from lack of sleep, and his chronic discomfort about not being able to make a decision were tangible reminders of how stuck and anxious he'd been; although life in Costa Rica brought all kinds of new challenges into his life, he perceived them as exciting because of what an improvement they were from the situation he'd been in before. Those visceral memories formed what is known as an internal baseline that enabled the contrast effect to occur. He was hyperaware of the positive feedback he was getting from the children and families he was hired to help, and also extremely sensitive to how good he felt doing all the things that had pushed him out of his comfort zone. This awareness made him feel more trusting and confident in his ability to take on new challenges.

And this is exactly the awareness and motivation that fueled his ultimate shift in mindset, not just as a temporary fix, but in a way that he could own it—now and forever.

· ANNE: HOW TO NURTURE AN ACTIVIST MINDSET ·

Anne is seventy-eight years young. A native Californian, she plays tennis year-round, is active in real estate, swims, and does yoga. She goes out three or four evenings a week—dinner with a friend or two, to the library to hear an interesting speaker, to the movies or theater. She's always loved being physically active, enjoying how it makes her feel healthy, energetic, and "on top of her game." But now something has begun to change; she is often irritable, feels easily overwhelmed by things she used to take in stride, and worst of all, feels like she can't do anything about her situation. Even though she has two daughters who love her and want to take care of her, she pushes them away, resenting the intrusion. Her daughters try to convince her that she is doing too much and needs to slow down.

Anne insists that "I've always been this way. This is just the way

I am." But in quieter moments, she knows something is up. Lately she's finding that she's pushing herself out the door; she resents the invitations and dreads the events on her calendar. Anne continues to believe that all this activity is good for her—this has been the precise strategy that has worked for decades. She had to stay active in order to manage her anxiety. Yes, she admits to herself, her body and brain are slowing down due to aging, but if she lets go and starts to change any one of these relied-upon habits, all hell will break loose. In fact, she's terrified to stop moving.

It's probably easy for you to see from the outside looking in that Anne would benefit from slowing things down a bit: rest more, balance physical activity with slow-moving relaxation exercises, not push herself to go out so often in the evenings. But what's got her stuck is her belief that her activities define who she is. If she stops, won't she just go to pieces? So she pushes on, afraid to make any changes.

These habits—exercise, a busy social life, and an engaging job—are what she has always relied on to feel purposeful and centered. She didn't really associate them with lessening her anxiety for the years that she was maintaining her busy schedule. But now that her activity level is being threatened, she does feel anxious and as if she is losing control of her life. Her busyness has helped her cope with anxiety for years, buffering against the stress. Now she has to slow down and look at what these changes are really saying: that she has become more anxious.

Like many of us, Anne did not want to admit that she felt anxious. Her idea of herself was very much anchored by feeling physically and emotionally vital and even-keeled. But when Anne got sick with pneumonia, she was finally forced to slow down. Yes, she felt terrible. She could barely lift her head off the pillow and all she wanted to do was sleep for about two weeks. But this slowing down had a silver lining: It forced Anne to admit how weak she felt and how anxious she'd been feeling for a while.

For Anne, the flare-up of anxiety was a warning signal that it was time for a change. She hated feeling so depleted and decided her daughters might have a good point; what used to feel good didn't anymore. She decided to embrace the slowdown just to give it a try. Her illness gave her a good excuse. She could tell how the longer and deeper sleep that came with her recovery made her feel just a bit better every day. She also decided to explore what amount of sleep would make her feel best once she was fully recovered instead of just going back to her old habits. She noticed that she actually felt a hit of relief not to have to be out with friends all the time, attending lectures and dinners and galas. By creating some space between herself and her activities, she was able to take the time to reassess whether she was seeing them for what they were or seeing them for what they used to mean to her before her situation shifted. She gave herself permission to realize that the downtime felt good and helped her feel stronger. She decided instead of immediately going back to her social schedule, she would pick and choose those events that she was really excited to attend, which would automatically whittle down the number of engagements on her calendar. She did start to feel an itch to get back to regular physical activity and believed that was a good sign, but there too she decided her strategy was going to be experimental rather than prescriptive. She was going to slowly add back tennis, one day at a time, and let her body tell her when the number of games per week was enough.

....

In this case, Anne was forced to relearn a valuable lesson: We are constantly changing beings, and we need to be attuned to our changes in order to adapt. Trying to doggedly stick to an old routine just because she had always done it that way was hurting Anne, but her fear was preventing her from taking the time she needed to reassess and make a new plan. She had discovered a core idea behind the activist mindset: *When you believe you are able to adapt, you will feel yourself thrive while you adapt*. Her daughters could not believe the change in Anne—she had always been a force of nature and still was, but the new elements of deep self-awareness, optimism, and her belief that she could still learn gave her an added confidence to make her life wonderful—especially at the ripe young age of seventy-eight. Indeed, Anne discovered another advantage to the superpower of mindset—the power of self-experimentation. She found that when she listened to her body and tried different things to optimize its response, she not only knew what her body needed but felt more in control of her health. In the end, this realization may have been the best gift she could give herself: "Nobody is going to call me an old dog who can't learn new tricks."

· LIZA: DON'T JUST PRESS MUTE ON THE WHAT-IF PLAYLIST ·

Sometimes our go-to coping mechanisms can tell us a lot about how well—or not—we are doing handling the stress of daily living. It's important to keep in mind that there's a difference between coping mechanisms that simply mask the problem and don't actually do anything to penetrate it and healthy coping mechanisms that we intentionally adapt over time because we or our circumstances change. Accessing your activist mindset necessitates being both objective and positive. It also requires developing awareness of your anxiety triggers and the ensuing negative feelings.

Take Liza's situation, for example. You may recall how she was running every morning before heading to the office, pushing herself at work, and then ending her day crashed on the couch, an empty wine bottle by her side. On her good days, she got away with this routine. But over time, these coping mechanisms were no longer as effective. Indeed, it was as if she'd hit a roadblock, in which her go-to strategies were now interfering with her life. She felt like a failure. And the feedback she was getting at work was all bad: "You bring everyone's mood down"; "too controlling"; and "harsh on everyone around her."

Liza could barely recognize herself. She knew she didn't feel good, but she didn't know why—and she was afraid that if she looked too closely at the problem, her whole world would fall apart with no hope of being rebuilt. She would wake up in the middle of the night with a long list of "what-ifs"—everything she could possibly think of that could go wrong at work. She was feeling slightly paranoid about her colleagues, imagining that different people were trying to undermine her role or take projects away from her. The only relief she had from the obsessive thoughts in her head was at the end of the long workday, when she'd come home to her wine. For a brief two or three hours, the alcohol would push away all the self-doubts about her performance at work, all the worries that one mistake would mean she'd lose her job, and all the fears about her future. It was as if she'd pressed mute on her problems.

In a sweat and with her heart racing, she would ask herself, *What happened to my confidence? Why have I become such a raving bi***?* Her irritability and her difficulty managing it were a clear signal to her that something was changing.

In order to right her ship, she had to first begin by acknowledging how her behaviors were no longer helping with her anxiety; she had to admit she had to curb or stop her drinking. Then she looked for support to help understand how and when her anxiety began to become too big for her to handle. Finally, when Liza began eliminating the wine at night, she began to get better sleep. This first step was key because it calmed down her nervous system and brought her into more balance. From that steadier position, Liza was able to consider what in her environment needed to be reassessed. She knew she was in a bad rut at work. What Liza wanted most of all was that buzz of excitement, that thrill of loving her work and pushing her body. The high she'd get from working on a productive team. So she asked her boss to put her on a new project, with a new set of people—this would allow her to hit the reset button on how she was working. Liza also asked whether she could do some outside professional development with a private coach. These changes re-upped her interest and motivation at work. The coach helped Liza identify how resetting her mindset could completely transform her work life. For example, Liza was able to see that she hadn't always been so hard on herself, and that negative self-talk was contributing to her feelings of frustration and fear at work. Shifting her mindset allowed her a kinder and gentler attitude toward herself and her work performance and goals. As an added bonus, this new attitude naturally expanded to everyone around her in her work world. She learned how to adopt a more open-ended frame of mind: She no longer felt so compelled to control every aspect of her workday lest she be deemed less valuable. She did not always have to be in charge. She could also learn to relax and listen.

Our outlook on life and attitude toward our own experience are important facets of our overall well-being, health, and happiness. As you consider what you want to change about your attitude toward yourself and your life, begin to play with one or more of the hacks below. Let yourself experiment in an open-ended way by adopting the position of a scientist. And trust that more than likely when you adopt this new optimistic stance, you will feel better. This reward alone will reinforce a new, more life-enhancing attitude network. In essence, Liza created an activist mindset.

· A ROSE BY ANY OTHER NAME ·

As I was working on this chapter, I asked myself the question "Is there such a thing as too much reframing?"

I was thinking about my friend Celine, a brilliant journalist, author, and entrepreneur who once told me she had never in her life been rejected for a writing piece.

"Wow," I said to her a bit tongue in cheek, "I knew people who went to Harvard were really smart, but I had no idea they had magical powers like this!"

She quickly explained that she had never been rejected because each submission had resulted in a positive step forward. That is, either she made a deeper connection with an editor, acquired some useful feedback (including "Dear Celine, Your piece was a load of c**p. Best regards, The Editor"), or discovered a new direction for the piece itself. She saw each one of these outcomes as a "win" and NOT a rejection.

Now that's some powerful reframing. But it made me ask myself, Is there such a thing as too much reframing? Does excessive reframing ever cross over into "fooling yourself," where your friends and family have the desire to step in to intervene? I asked myself these questions because I believe that I learn more from my failures and rejections than I do from my slam-dunk successes. Of course success feels a whole lot better, but success just gives you more of the same data: what's working well. As a scientist, a grant writer, a speaker for hire, and now an entrepreneur, I love when I have success—but I know that I learn from failure. Reframing is a tool for viewing failure through a productive lens, not erasing failure to the point that you never learn. In the end, I like to label a slam dunk a slam dunk, and a stinky failure a stinky failure—either way, both are a reflection of how I work, although not a reflection of my total value as a person. While I allow myself to feel the sting of a failure, rejection, or negotiation that did not go my way, I try to focus on what that failure can teach me: What did I understand? How should I modify my current plan or revise my goal? In this way I am able to use negative experiences as learning tools but am still allowing myself to feel the full range of my emotions.

· MOVING YOUR ACTIVIST MINDSET INTO HIGH GEAR ·

An activist mindset is not a secret gift that only a few lucky people possess. It truly is a skill that is learned with practice over time. And like any habit in our lives, the more we practice it, the stronger and more automatic it becomes. The element of practice is precisely why those of us who suffer from anxiety have a clear advantage at developing this superpower. Why? Because reassessment can only come when you are aware of what's not working for you, and anxiety is the emotion that pinpoints exactly that.

A stubborn source of anxiety for me used to be my fear of being seen for who I really was on the inside. I felt like if I revealed any imperfections, insecurities, or negative aspects, I would not be successful or even accepted. This was a difficult fear to uproot because it was so much a part of how I thought about myself; if I let any cracks show, the whole house could come tumbling down. Instead of admitting this fear, I would dodge it—a classic kind of avoidant behavior. How would I dodge it? I just used the old adage "Fake it till you make it" and told myself that my "fake" would turn into a "make" if I just believed it hard enough. The problem for me was that I got really good at masking the frustration, anger, and disagreement instead of focusing on communicating them clearly and authentically. My real fear was that no one would want to know the "real" me with all the frustration, anger, complaining, and imperfection that comes with living your life.

I also realized that part of my own form of bad anxiety came with not allowing myself to express any of these very natural negative emotions and instead just bottling them up or only releasing them in a very limited situation. I needed to realize that I was doing this to myself, not because there were any true consequences to expressing those negative sentiments. It took time for me to recognize that it was unhealthy not to let myself express these negative emotions in public. I'm not talking about having a temper tantrum, just expressing normal anger if something does not go right or a colleague or associate is a real jerk—of course I have the right to be angry and frustrated. Admitting that I sometimes got angry at a colleague or even my mom was a huge step toward accepting all of myself, even my anxiety. It also let me see that these negative emotions were not a deficit I had but were in fact giving me information about relationships and situations that needed more attention.

It's taken quite a while to realize the depths of how I have suppressed those negative emotions and in doing so suppressed myself. But I now have a much healthier mindset about my emotions and how to express them, and in that way reveal my true self to the world.

I now consider this insight to be one of my superpowers. There is no better motivator to tell you what you need to work on than your own array of anxiety triggers. They can be a path forward to some of the best realizations and shifts you can make in your life today.

Anxiety gives us a constant supply of reasons to engage our activist mindsets in both big and small ways. By allowing ourselves space to observe our negative feelings, our fears, and our insecurities, we are actually giving ourselves a chance to identify ways we can strengthen our foundation. Engaging an activist mindset to examine anxiety with the intention of building that skill up will get you to superpower status. Think back on the profiles in this chapter. Anne's anxiety was telling her she needed to reexamine her schedule, and by ignoring that anxiety she ended up getting ill. It was only once she was forced to slow down that she was able to use her activist mindset to see that her tolerance for social and physical activity was changing. After her illness, she had to refocus that mindset on the present and realized that what was going to work for her now was different from what had worked great five or even ten years earlier. She developed the real superpower of an activist mindset that she enjoys deploying at will. Jared learned that by creating space between himself and his negative emotions he was able to reframe his perception of himself. Liza, too, needed to give herself permission to face the source of her anxiety before she was able to address the root causes. Once she did, she was able to achieve an even deeper level of satisfaction. Too often we allow fear to overshadow the more subtle, nuanced message that anxiety is trying to send. But if you can take a beat to observe what that anxiety is trying to show you, you give yourself the potential to make an activist mindset your own not-so-secret superpower.

7

Amplify Your Focus and Productivity

The relationship between anxiety and attention is like any meaningful relationship—it's complicated. Bad anxiety is that wily beast that steals our focus, makes our thoughts distracting, and gets in the way of getting things done. We become vulnerable to what I call our annoying what-if list that wakes us in the middle of the night and drags us down a rabbit hole.

- What if I don't get that raise?
- What if he/she/they don't like me?
- What if I can't make the rent?
- What if I can't land that next deal?
- What if my kid doesn't get into their dream school?
- What if somebody gets sick?

The what-if list can go on ad infinitum. And yet, is the what-if list (i.e., worry) always bad? Is it always a negative side effect of anxiety? Yes and no.

Science has shown that bad anxiety disrupts the attention network (see page 133), causing distractibility and difficulty sustaining focus on a task. However, research has also shown that highly anxious people (those, for instance, suffering from generalized anxiety disorder) often exhibit a kind of hyperfocus. Because high anxiety can stem from an oversensitive threat response, people become hypervigilant and super-focused on danger—real or imagined. This hyperfocus then extends to all aspects of their lives. For example, recently researchers[1] had people with a clinical diagnosis of generalized anxiety disorder and nonclinically anxious individuals perform a test of attention that measures aspects of all three attentional networks (i.e., the alerting, orienting, and executive control networks; see below for further details). Each group performed this task under either what is called high cognitive load (a form of cognitive "stress" such as counting backward from one hundred by threes) or low cognitive load (counting backward from one hundred by ones). They found that when a person is both highly anxious with GAD and performing under high cognitive load, their GAD can actually help their attention become more precise; the focus necessary to manage the cognitive load demands more from the attention network. But generally, we know that if the cognitive load is too high, our attention will become less efficient.

This interaction between attention, thinking, and emotion is played out in what we call *executive function*—all those skills we rely on when we manage information in our heads while under the stress of daily living and trying to simply get things done. But the reverse is also true: When anxious people are less occupied (i.e., under low cognitive load, no stress, or no stimulation) they become more vulnerable to their worry, and therefore more distracted.

We all have a sweet spot of good anxiety, a body-brain space where we feel engaged, alert, and just stressed enough to maximize our attention and focus on what we want to do. In this state, we can stay on task, hone in on projects or deadlines, and ultimately be more productive. Caught in too much anxiety we become more vulnerable: On the one hand, we run the risk of being distracted; on the other, we risk becoming so hyperfocused on threats that we lose the ability to evaluate whether a threat is real and worth our time or imagined and not worth worrying about. Our challenge becomes learning how to keep focused on our prize (whatever goal that may be) while resisting distractions or unhelpful hyperfocus. Indeed, it's a kind of "high-wire" act that gets better with practice. What does this mean for those of us looking for ways to channel our anxiety into something productive? We need to learn how to cultivate our what-if lists.

The big news here is that you can learn to shift the restless energy behind the what-if list and not only control your focus but improve your productivity. This is a form of channeling your anxiety. Further, many of the strategies that can amplify and support focus and productivity can also be used to flip anxiety from bad to good, creating a positive feedback loop in your brain-body that keeps on giving, regardless of any turmoil in your life or bad-anxiety flare-ups. How? The attention network's key features incorporate or rely on executive control, which you may recall plays an important role in regulating our emotions—a key step to calming anxiety. Let's take a closer look at the underlying neurobiology.

· THE BASICS OF EXECUTIVE FUNCTION AND THE ATTENTION SYSTEM ·

Broadly speaking, executive function includes the attention system and can be broken down into three distinct areas:

- Inhibition or inhibitory control is one of the more basic executive functions that relate to our ability to manage attention and core emotions. Essentially, it's the capacity to think before you act—this ability to resist the urge to say or do something allows us the time to evaluate a situation and how our behavior might impact it. Inhibitory control also enables sustained attention—the capacity to maintain attention on a situation or task in spite of distractibility, fatigue, or boredom. When this function is mature, people are able to wait their turn patiently and resist an outburst if someone cuts them in line. The child who has trouble inhibiting control is the one who has more trouble resisting taking a second marshmallow when the teacher is out of the room. The adolescent or adult who has trouble in this area might not be able to manage anger and could even reach a point where they react with physical violence with very little provocation. Anxiety—especially when chronic—can exacerbate inhibitory control, making it more difficult for us to have some top-down control over intense emotions.

- Working memory is like a memory cloud that is held near enough for the person to actively retrieve information when needed. As adults, our working memory comes into play as we organize our day, keep on task, and get work done all at the same time. It incorporates the ability to draw on past learning or experience to apply to the situation at hand or to project into the future. Working memory is distinct from short-term memory and refers to the dynamic process of holding information in mind while performing complex tasks. Working memory should not be confused with long-term memory dependent on the hippocampus, but it is just as essential. The best way to think about working memory is as the kind of memory you use to keep relevant information in mind as you plan your next steps. For example, in the popular series *The Queen's Gambit*, the main character, chess prodigy Beth Harmon, often visualizes the chessboard on the ceiling, studying her options before making her next move. That ability to keep the current board layout "in mind" while choosing your next move is a great (though highly advanced) example of working memory. Never fear: While many of us are not able to keep all thirty-two chess pieces in mind while planning our next move like Beth, we can keep the name of someone new we just met in mind during the conversation—another common example of working memory.

Anxiety can impinge on working memory, lessening its ability. We can all relate to those moments when under stress or when afraid we forget what we wanted to say, or our memory of a name disappears from our brain. The name is not actually gone, but our working memory has lost the ability to access it in that particular moment.

- Cognitive flexibility: In a basic way, cognitive flexibility is the ability to switch from one task to another when the goal or circumstances have changed. Through a more conceptual lens, cognitive flexibility refers to the ability to revise plans in the face of obstacles, setbacks, new information, or mistakes. It's the kind of "roll with the punches" idea whereby we are flexible enough to adapt to changing conditions. No doubt, this is both a mental and an emotional ability. In research related to the relationship between

> anxiety and cognitive flexibility, scientists have looked at how highly anxious people can be cognitively inflexible. But just as our response to anxiety can vary, so, too, can our ability to switch tasks and adapt to changing circumstances. Remember when we described being able to reframe or reappraise a situation? Being able to look at a mistake or failure as information instead of an indictment of our abilities? This shift in mindset is an example of cognitive flexibility.

Executive functions are carried out by a wide range of brain areas centered in the prefrontal cortex right behind the forehead, but also an even larger number of brain areas, some of which are shown below.

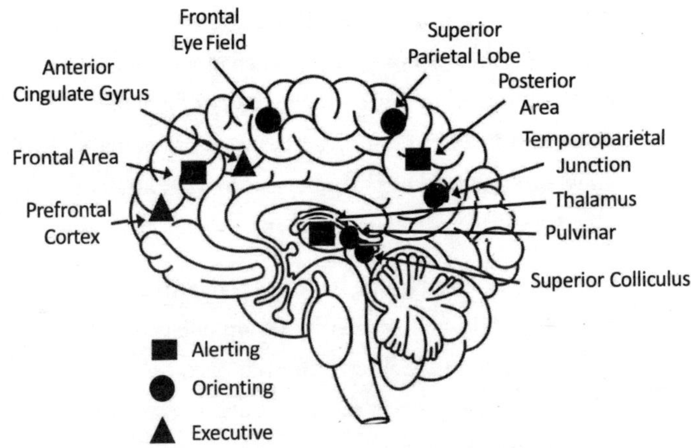

Figure 5. The larger set of brain structures that underlie different aspects of attention. Major impairments in attention are seen with damage to the prefrontal cortex (to the left in this brain diagram), but you can see that a much wider network of brain structures is involved in focusing and maintaining attention. (Taken from Petersen and Posner.[2])

Figure 6.

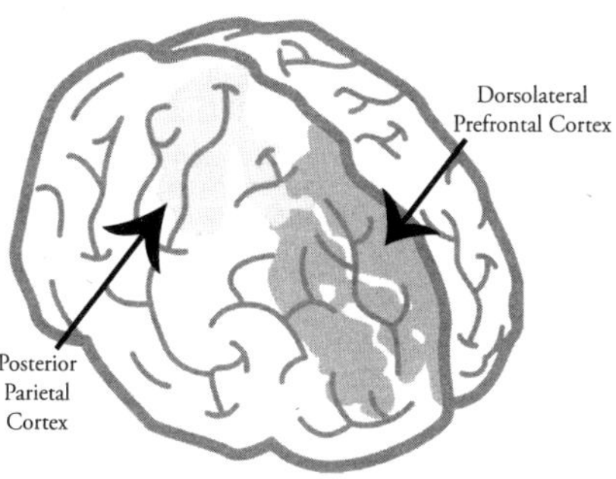

It used to be thought that highly anxious people simply had impaired executive control and difficulty regulating their emotions. But recent studies have fine-tuned our understanding of exactly how anxiety impacts attention in general, and executive control in particular.

The attention system[3] is generally defined as comprising three separate but related networks that correspond to several anatomical areas: 1) the **alerting** network helps us maintain an appropriate level of awareness to stimuli in our environment, whether this is visual or emotional in nature, and their potential to be dangerous (this is related to our built-in threat response); 2) the **orienting** system is in charge of selecting what stimuli to attend to. In other words, orienting network information and decides what is important and what is not; 3) the **executive control** network is the complex web of interactions in charge of exerting top-down control over any situation; it's this third system that affects how we process anxiety.

Executive function, the mental skills at the intersection of attention, thinking, and emotion, is that "top-down" brain system or network that is part of how we control and channel emotions such as anxiety. We use our executive functions to get things done, stay organized and on task, and manage the ups and downs of our feelings. If this system is overtaxed by stressors (too many deadlines, too little rest), our ability to manage these functions dwindles. Scientists call this dimension of executive functioning "an effortful process"—it doesn't happen automatically; it requires deliberate, conscious thought. We need some arousal (i.e., good anxiety) to motivate this effort; but too much arousal or stimulation can shut down the effort.

· KYLIE: WHY MULTITASKING MAY NOT WORK FOR YOU ·

Kylie is a typical fifteen-year-old who is never without her smartphone. She uses it to text her closest friends, follow her wider circle of friends and acquaintances, play games on her many apps, and occasionally check her email—if only to look for assignment changes from her teachers. She's always been an active kid who plays soccer for two hours every day after school, sleeps well at night (her mother is particularly attentive to Kylie's needing about eight to nine hours per night), and seems otherwise well adjusted—except that now she's been feeling increasingly anxious.

She's also having trouble sleeping and she's noticed a dip in her grades, which makes her feel worse about herself. She is working just as hard as she usually does, and she's talked to her teachers to see if there is any area that can be improved. Her mother has identified the most likely culprit for this decline: multitasking. Kylie has been insisting that she can focus better when she's listening to music or by sometimes taking breaks and "window shopping" on her phone. "It helps me relax," she explains. But her mother has been doing her own homework, discovering that adolescent brains are in a drawn-out period of change and increased plasticity. In fact, the adolescent brain is so dynamic that these changes are not all about adding neurons (neurogeneration) but also about pruning (i.e., removing unneeded connections).

In early childhood, the brain is on fire creating new neurons and synapses. When we hit adolescence, it's time for pruning to begin—this is the brain's way of tidying up and getting rid of synapses that are not being used, to help it become more efficient. This pruning mainly takes place in the prefrontal cortex and the adjacent parietal lobe, the areas so important to executive functions including decision making. As this process occurs, there are many unused, extra synapses floating around. This explains why teenagers often make irrational decisions or show questionable judgment—their executive systems are in flux and wild disarray!

With Kylie's uptick in stimuli—the near-constant texting, Snapchatting, and social media views—she's increasing the demands on her executive functioning. In other words, her brain really can't keep up with all the stimulation and the inner changes going on at the same time. Why is this significant? Because she feels more anxious. The increased anxiety is a signal that she's out of balance.

Does the nonceasing overstimulation create the anxiety, or does anxiety simply become more noticeable and intense because of the overstimulation? It's a bit of a chicken-and-egg problem and both are true. But the end result is the same: She is distracted, is less productive, and feels increasingly ill at ease with herself. The biggest takeaway, especially from Kylie's mom's point of view, is that her typically grounded daughter seems to have lost control of her ability to manage her online life, school, sports, and emotions. From my point of view, Kylie's anxiety has heightened and her executive functioning has lessened.

More than likely Kylie may be able to multitask more efficiently in a few years, after this pruning stage is complete. However, for now, it's best that she put away her distractions so that she feels better able to narrow her attention and get back on track with her schoolwork. When her mother insists that she put her phone in another room while she does her homework and restricts online access, Kylie's mood begins to shift. Kylie even has to admit that without her phone nearby, she feels better about school and also less anxious. It is no surprise to her mother or to her that her grades soon recover from their dip.

If we were to look at her brain using functional magnetic resonance imaging (fMRI), we would more than likely see how her attention network was being hijacked whenever she got distracted by her phone, for whatever reason. The shift in her attention was enough to disrupt the circuit, which then triggered anxious feelings.[4]

Kylie's story shows how our attention system can so easily be impacted by outside forces. It also shows how distraction and other interruptions in executive functioning can trigger anxiety or exacerbate it. In Kylie's case, she (and her mom) discovered an easy, if temporary, fix. The key going forward would be to continue paying attention to what works best for Kylie in managing her anxiety, and what kinds of distractions push her cognitive load and upset the balance.

When anxiety increases and begins to overwhelm our brain-body, tipping us over into bad-anxiety mode, running interference and resetting our balance can be more complicated. In Kylie's case, she wasn't really affected long term so her reset was simple: When she took away the distracting technology, her focus returned and her anxiety lessened. But in this age of constant tech-ing, it's all too possible to create deeper, more sinister relationships with or reliance on technology. This is problematic not only in terms of distraction and executive functioning (loss of inhibitory control and strain on working memory) but it creeps into other neural pathways, including those related to reward, and then can take on an addictive nature. (I will go into more detail about how addictive relationships with substances and other sources of reward and self-soothing have much more significant implications.)

Regardless of your age, however, research shows that multitasking puts a strain on working memory, concentration, and deep thinking. Have you ever been having a conversation while driving and suddenly found yourself lost or taking the wrong exit? Or what about reading emails while on a conference call? We think we can attend to and process both but we can't. The lesson here that is backed by both psychology and neuroscience is this: Multitasking can put too much of a cognitive load on our executive functions, which can trigger or worsen anxiety. The other side of this coin is that sometimes paying active attention to the source of our distractions, keeping our focus and attention more narrow or singular, can not only improve productivity even during challenging situations but also lessen a bout of bad anxiety.

But as we know, anxiety can be tricky. The problem of dealing with anxiety is not always lack of focus or attention; anxiety can also go hand in hand with a hyperfocused attention on that what-if list that won't let up.

· GAIL: LEARNING NEW WAYS TO TRAIN HER ATTENTION AND FOCUS ·

Gail is in her early fifties and has recently gone back to work after many years at home raising her three children. When all three of her children moved out of the house to pursue college and develop their careers, she decided to get a job. She found a job as an office manager for a busy dental practice. For the first two years she looked forward to the work, her colleagues, and her paycheck. She liked that her working meant her husband did not have to put in as many long hours at his job. Indeed, one of her goals was to save what she earned so that they could enjoy each other's company and take more trips together.

But then things started to change.

Here was a person whom her husband, Ron, called the ever-ready bunny—someone who got up at dawn every morning for an early-morning walk, took care of the kids, made three meals a day, volunteered, carpooled, was active in her church group, you name it; she could do it all with one hand tied behind her back. And when she returned to work, she continued to be a master of efficiency and productivity. Slowly but steadily, however, she began to lose her oomph, as she called it. Gail began having trouble falling asleep and staying asleep. She began to suffer from a mounting, gnawing anxiety. "I'm so moody," she described, "and my anxiety is off the charts. I just don't feel like myself anymore." She tired more easily, and in general felt the life go out of her bones. "It's as if a ten-ton elephant is sitting on my chest—I'm flattened out and unable to move."

Gail was willing to live with her fatigue and even her moodiness. But when she began to feel completely unable to focus at work, that was the last straw. She went to see her doctor, who explained that anxiety and trouble sleeping are common side effects of menopause. This information did not surprise Gail—it had been almost two years since she'd last menstruated. Her doctor explained that there is a connection between dwindling estrogen levels and an overall decline in cognitive function, which often shows up as a difficulty staying focused. Gail was so estrogen-deficient that her physician suggested she could benefit from supplementing with bioidentical hormone supplements (hormone replacement therapy, or HRT), which could help alleviate her symptoms. Since she had no history of breast cancer in her family and all the recent research on HRT showed no negative side effects and only benefits, including protection against heart disease and a general offsetting of aging, she decided she had nothing to lose. She was especially motivated to try HRT because her doctor more or less promised that she would sleep better, her anxiety would lessen or disappear altogether, and her energy would return.

Is anxiety a common side effect of estrogen deficiency? Yes. Menopause is exactly that—a lessening or deficiency in production of estrogen, the central hormone produced by women. It's this estrogen deficiency that is associated with an increase in anxiety, sleep impairment, and an overall decrease in energy. Many women also complain of feeling more distracted, scattered, and having less focus—just like Gail. And estrogen supplementation can and does reverse that sense of splintered attention.

Gail did feel better when she started HRT, but she still felt only about 75 percent of her former focus. The turning point for Gail was an article she read about strategies for how to train your attention. There were three things on that list that have substantial scientific backing—meditation, cognitive training, and exercise—and she was determined to add all three to her regular list of activities because she didn't just want to get back to her old level; she wanted to see if she could actually improve her everyday focus and attention.

What was number one on Gail's list? She began to meditate regularly. She started there because it just made sense to her based on what she already knew about meditation.

· THE POWER OF MEDITATION ·

There is clear, well-established scientific support that meditation can remedy both hyperfocus and fractured attention.[5] Neuroscientists have been studying the impact of meditation on the brain, and in particular on attention processes. In studies by Dr. Richard Davidson and his colleagues[6], they looked at three different types of meditation: focused-attention meditation, in which the meditator focuses on the breath (inhalation and exhalation) as a means of sustaining attention rather than letting the mind wander; open-monitoring meditation, in which the meditator becomes aware of and open to all sensory stimuli picked up; and compassion and loving-kindness meditation, in which the meditator directs loving, compassionate thoughts toward others and the universe at large. All three types of meditation impact different areas of the brain. Compassion and loving-kindness meditation activates the temporoparietal junction (the intersection between the temporal and parietal lobes of your brain), for instance, and produces empathetic thoughts (i.e., putting oneself in another's shoes). Open-monitoring meditation affects the amygdala and other areas of the limbic system and shows evidence of decreasing anxiety and feelings of anger and fear. Focused-attention meditation affects the anterior cingulate cortex, which is involved in self-regulation and error detection; studies have shown that focused-attention meditation increases the ability to find the correct answer to well-defined problems. All of these have been shown to lessen anxiety and improve the ability to regulate emotion.

The key findings show that mindfulness meditation, integrative body-mind training such as yoga or tai chi, as well as simple exposure to nature can improve attention and emotion regulation. For example, one study[7] showed that three months of intensive meditation training improved an attention-based visual detection task in healthy adults. Another study[8] showed that integrative body-mind training (a practice adopted from Traditional Chinese Medicine that incorporates aspects of mindfulness meditation), done for just five days for twenty minutes per day in undergraduate students, improved performance on standard tasks of inhibitory control called the Eriksen flanker task, where you have to focus on a letter of the alphabet with a wide range of visual distractions. Recall that inhibitory control is one of the three core executive functions described at the beginning of this chapter. The control group in this study did relaxation training for the same amount of time. The group that did the meditation practice also had lower levels of anxiety, depression, anger, and fatigue and reported higher levels of vigor and reduced stress, measured by cortisol levels. This study suggests how this kind of body-mind training helps people develop a state of restful alertness that enables a higher degree of awareness, which ultimately improves behavior. The best news is that there is now a wide range of meditation apps all designed to get novice meditators going today.

We have a good idea how meditation can affect the brain from studies done on expert and novice meditators. Indeed, expert meditators show higher activations of the brain areas involved in the attention network relative to novice meditators. It was also noted (perhaps not surprisingly) that the expert meditators were less distractable during meditation than the novice meditators. Similar anatomical differences are seen in attention-related brain areas in the expert relative to novice meditators with some studies showing that these structural differences can be detected with just eight weeks of meditation training. This suggests that we don't have to isolate ourselves on a mountaintop and practice months of silent meditation at a time to start to see these effects. Even eight weeks of training in a novice meditator can start to produce brain changes that could improve your attention network. These are exactly the kind of changes Gail was likely enjoying after her own personal meditation training regimen.

· PHYSICAL ACTIVITY AND ATTENTION ·

As you now know, I'm a real believer in the power of exercise to change the brain. My studies show that physical activity improves attention and offsets anxiety. Even a single bout of exercise can improve attention and executive performance on a Stroop task.[9] In this task known to all students of psychology, you are asked to name the color that the text is printed in for a series of words. The trick is that all the words name different colors (e.g., red, green, yellow). When the word color (RED) matches the color of the text (i.e., it's printed in red text), it's easy and we name the color of the text very quickly. But if the word color (YELLOW) is printed in green text, we take much longer to say green. The ability to ignore the word and focus on the color is called selective attention and is dependent on the prefrontal cortex. Performance on this task improves after a single exercise session and long-term changes in your exercise regimen can cause long-lasting improvements in performance of this task as well.[10]

Ask anyone who is a regular exerciser and they are likely to report how they not only notice an improved overall mood and higher levels of energy post-workout but feel more focused as well. I know that after a workout session (which I now do exclusively in the mornings), I maximize my focus for writing or for tackling the most challenging items on my to-do list. I always feel better prepared to dig into whatever project is "on deck" after I've gotten my morning workout in.

Exercise improves many aspects of brain functioning. Like meditation, regular aerobic exercise has powerful positive effects on anxiety and depression, with one study showing that exercise can be as effective as one of the most popular antidepressants in treating major depressive disorder.[11] Exercise has been shown to reduce the symptoms of anxiety disorders and address the underlying neural functioning.[12]

One study reported that three months of increased aerobic exercise in older adults resulted in an increased volume of white matter, the output structure of the brain cells that convey information to the downstream cells.[13] While the precise mechanism for how prefrontal function improves and white matter volume increases has not been completely worked out, the increase in concentration of a whole range of growth factors in the brain is likely part of the answer. On a practical note, because even one exercise session (especially one lasting at least thirty minutes designed to get your heart rate up) has been shown to improve attention/executive function,[14] and anyone even in street clothes can get their heart rate up with a good power walk, physical activity is one of the fastest, easiest, and overall most convenient ways to buffer your own anxiety and boost your focus and attention.

One of the most mind-blowing observations I have made happened almost as a second thought. I was giving a thirty-minute live but virtual talk (via Zoom) to a bunch of incoming freshmen at

NYU and decided I wanted to make the talk memorable. I asked them all to exercise with me for the last ten minutes of class so they could truly "feel" the effects of exercise on their mood and cognitive function. At the last minute, I thought it would be interesting to measure their anxiety levels by having them do a very quick but standardized anxiety test before and after the workout and offer to send them their results after the lecture. I found high levels of anxiety in the group before the exercise, but after the exercise a whopping fifteen-point drop in the anxiety scores, which brought them to normal levels. For me, that shows the power of adding just ten minutes of movement to your life.

· VERONICA: QUANTIFY ELITE ATHLETE PERFORMANCE ·

The most memorable exercise subject I ever had in my lab was an NYU student whom I'll call Veronica. Veronica had asked to volunteer in my lab (something that happens regularly throughout the year). She told me she was training for the Olympics in pairs skating and wanted to study the effects of exercise on the brain. We were just getting one of our very first exercise studies up and running in the lab; we were looking at how an exercise session might impact a participant's ability to complete a worksheet that engaged the prefrontal cortex. The assignment was to draw a line between progressively increasing and alternating letters and numbers. For example, letters and numbers are printed randomly on the page, and you need to find the "1" and draw a line from the "1" to the "A" to the "2" to the "B" and so on until you run out of time. You have to search for and remember the locations of these letters and numbers and also keep track of the correct sequence. This task requires both attention to the array of letters and numbers and to the progression through the sequences as well as working memory, which is also called "scratchpad memory" and allows you to keep the memory of where you saw the "8" or the "K" in mind as you are going through the sequences. The job I gave Veronica was to be our exercise test subject—since I knew the fifty-minute exercise-bike workout that was part of the study would not be a problem for her. Not surprisingly, she did it easily. But what was really memorable was what happened next. I had never before nor have I since seen someone do that task of focused attention as fast or as accurately as she did. It was like Veronica was a focus machine—and she had never done that task before. I watched her quickly scan the whole page, and when I said "Go" she already had a good idea of where all the letters were. I could almost see how they would animate this if it were a scene of Sherlock Holmes doing this task.

What do you need to perform this task well? Now, I will fully admit that this is the one and only Olympic-level athlete I have tested in my lab, but it makes me want to test many more to see if this high level of prefrontal function is a general feature of similar Olympic-level athletes. What could be the reason? It could be that these athletes have to quickly assess their situation and get excellent training on mapping out their next move—I think about the amazing mogul and slalom skiers who need to map their line down the mountain with millisecond precision. It could be that part of their training, together with aerobic exercise, could be contributing to their efficiency. It could also be that her regular aerobic training has also improved her ability to channel the energy of arousal to improve her performance on this task. I can't know for sure with just a single person tested, but there are many exciting ideas to investigate!

· RECENT RESEARCH ON ATTENTION ·

One of the more recent areas of study on attention is focused on video game training and whether it undermines or improves attention and overall well-being. A 2018 review of research examined studies done on video games, including action games, as well as "brain-training" programs and puzzle games. Interestingly, *Tetris*, an addictive puzzle video game, was shown to be more effective than established brain-training programs at improving short-term memory and processing speed. Similarly, *Portal*, another popular puzzle-platform game, was found to be more effective at improving problem-solving skills than *Lumosity*, a well-regarded commercial brain-training program. Although the results of these studies varied somewhat depending on the age of the participants, game genre, and length of the experiment itself, the results were quite positive. Researchers seem to agree that video games may very well help children solidify executive function skills and healthy adults stem the tide of cognitive decline. The upshot? Video games and brain-training programs again point to the brain's plasticity and its ability to improve in functioning.[15]

· DEV: LEARNING TO USE ANXIETY IN A COMPLETELY NEW WAY ·

Dev was a successful entrepreneur. By thirty-two, he had already built and sold four successful companies, but his current company, a startup developing a new way to make airplane travel easier and more enjoyable, was stalling. (Of course this story happened way before COVID had shut down regional, national, and global travel!) He received a lot of early interest from investors because of his stellar reputation, but the sprint tests (i.e., fast and focused pushes where you put all your resources into going from idea to prototype product as fast as you can and test it with customers) he and his company had been doing were not developing as planned and he was having trouble raising his next round of funding. He was constantly flying between his offices in New York and LA to put fires out and felt like a chicken with his head cut off. As he described to me, his anxiety was out of control.

Dev had always loved the excitement and the fly-by-the-seat-of-your-pants-ness of the startup world and prided himself on being able to push past the pain and pressure to get the job done—that's when he could handle the stress and channel the arousal. But this time around he was beginning to fear that he just couldn't keep up. He hadn't been able to talk about his steadily creeping anxiety, and it was fast becoming an extra weight on him, making him doubt his last move—even when his logical mind and his gut both told him it was the right thing to do. He often fell into an incessant replay loop of that last conversation with the investor who turned him down, scrutinizing the conversation for all the points where he totally screwed up.

And now his funding was not coming through as he hoped. Anticipating a negative outcome, Dev felt his anxiety swelling like some overburdened swamp in a flood. His anxiety had turned from manageable to out of control.

One night, when Dev felt desperate, he texted a former colleague who had also played in the startup sandbox. He'd never asked her for advice, but he had witnessed her be a mentor to others. Dev trusted Monica and knew that she was someone he could talk to. Monica specialized in the business development end of things, having successfully worked with a long list of really successful startups including one or two Dev was involved in.

Monica called Dev within seconds of receiving his text.

Just hearing the sound of her voice calmed Dev. He brought to mind an image of her—always beautifully dressed and well prepared. He pushed himself to explain how he'd been feeling.

Then Monica shared a story about herself. She admitted to Dev that she had suffered from anxiety all her life. She used to obsess over every move and every last decision in her early years. It nearly made her search for a new way to make a living.

It was hard for Dev to believe this given her Wonder Woman persona.

But then Monica told Dev her secret. She said she realized that all her obsessive tendencies that led her to worry and question every move were actually a major advantage in her business and her life (note an activist mindset here). She realized that when she was under pressure (i.e., high cognitive load) to make a deal, she could train her attention to identify all the possible pitfalls in a particular situation. She realized that rather than blow off that instinct, she could actually use it to create a list of possible scenarios to analyze. This strategy worked for her business decisions and her life decisions. She realized that her what-if list wasn't actually a sign that she was losing her touch; it was a tool to help her do a more effective and complete evaluation of any business proposition at hand. Monica had stumbled on a trick for using the protective function of her anxiety in a whole new highly productive way to stay out of the bad zone. She became tuned in to those nervous jitters—not just expecting them but wanting them to help stoke her internal furnace. She had taught herself how to use the agitation of her good anxiety to drill down (top-down control of her attention system) on her business decisions and dealings. As she remarked to Dev, "Embracing my anxiety has made me a much more effective entrepreneur."

Dev saw immediately how he could use the same strategy to help focus his what-if list to better evaluate the negatives of any business situation that might arise and strengthen both his decision-making process and his arguments to clients and potential investors. This is how Dev "operationalized" Monica's strategy:

- He thought about his goal and what he wanted to achieve, including his worries and fears about whether or not he could accomplish the goal.

- Then he listed all the what-ifs that came to mind as possible obstacles to achieving his goal.
- Next, he made a list of all the actions he could take to address each of the what-ifs on the list. (Note that sometimes just listing out actions is a productive first step in considering all possible outcomes or scenarios of a particular situation.)
- Then he began to check off each action as he accomplished it.
- As he went through the list, he rewrote it, updating it.
- He repeated this exercise until he reached his goal.

This exercise became Dev's systematic strategy for dealing with his fears and experience of heightened anxiety around his business. But he soon discovered that it was a strategy he could apply to most of the challenges in his life—either personal or work-related. Instead of feeling roadblocked by his anxiety, he could channel his worries (aka his what-if list) into an action list, effectively transforming his anxiety into a superpower of productivity.

For Dev, this strategy made him feel like he gained a secret superpower. Whereas he once thought he would forever suffer from bad anxiety, he now realized he had the power to channel his hyperfocus on the business what-ifs into a powerful business strategy that he knew was going to start lifting him up very soon. As a result, Dev discovered a new confidence in himself. Whereas he used to hear a small voice question his decisions, he now trusted himself more. He knew that using his attention to detail not only helped him second-guess himself less but also made him feel more at ease. He also began to trust his instincts around innovation, not getting bogged down in whether every idea was going to be perfect. He knew that some ideas were going to make it; others would not. No big deal.

· BETTER FOCUS LEADS TO HEIGHTENED PRODUCTIVITY ·

We have focused this chapter on the neurobiology of attention, how to improve attention (with exercise and meditation), how the particular form of focused attention is a form of good anxiety (or in the case of Dev, it BECOMES a form of good anxiety), and that the reason to develop it in this way is that it leads directly to productivity.

For example, Dev's productivity increased immediately once he started using his what-if checklist to help him problem-solve any new product for his startup. Kyle's school performance improved by decreasing her distractions while she was doing her homework. And Gail was able to get back to her former ever-ready-bunny status with the help of her regular meditation practice to increase her ability to focus and sustain attention at work. (The estrogen supplements also helped!) Veronica's incredible performance on the scratch-pad memory (or working memory) test showed the effects of regular exercise on her focused attention. In all four cases the subjects used the underlying arousal of their negative anxiety and channeled it via the attention network. If they had not zeroed in on how the attention network functions, they would not have been able to channel or leverage the arousal of their anxiety. Further, when they took away the negative stimuli (in Kyle's case), calmed their brain-body systems (in Gail's and Dev's cases), or simply leaned into their ability to attend (in Veronica's case), they improved their capacity for attention. In other words, good anxiety improves attention if you can:

- decrease distractions
- meditate to improve focus and productivity
- exercise to stimulate both calm and alertness
- transform an anxiety-laden what-if list into a productive, goal-directed to-do list

8

Prime Your Social Brain, Quell Your Social Anxiety, and Heighten Your Compassion

Throughout our lives we use language and nonverbal communication tools to infer how others are feeling and to communicate our thoughts, feelings, desires, and intentions. From facial expressions to gestures, tone of voice to conversational style—all of these are learned behaviors that allow us to interact with and communicate within society. We develop and attune to the social norms of all the various social groups we belong to—from our family to our school to our workplace and our wider social circles. The more effective we are at these modes of interaction, the more in control of our lives we feel and the more successful we can be at navigating the world, careers, and personal relationships. Daniel Goleman coined the term "social intelligence" (also referred to as SQ for "social quotient") to describe our ability to navigate these social situations along with our emotions and argues that our SQ (as well as our emotional intelligence, also referred to as EQ) is even more important than IQ as a predictor of our personal and professional success. And these social skills play an important role in how we manage anxiety and learn to control it.

We begin to learn these skills immediately after birth. In the back-and-forth between an infant and a parent or caregiver, a baby first begins to pay attention to the incoming physical and emotional stimuli from his or her primary caregiver. A baby is wired to watch and respond to facial cues, eye contact of their mothers especially. This kind of interaction helps to establish healthy attachment, which is one of the most important foundations for healthy emotional and psychological development. Over a short amount of time, parent and child begin to coordinate their nonverbal communications in an automatic way—neuroscientists call this *social synchrony*—which lays down the foundation for how we interact well into the future. In fact, when this interaction is absent or inconsistent, children's cognitive and emotional development is impacted. Studies show correlation between this lack of parent-child interaction with lower IQ, and difficulty self-regulating, and long-term deficits in academic performance, including social skills.[1]

Our verbal and nonverbal communication abilities are an essential set of social cognitive skills that are anchored in our mammalian biology and tied to specific brain networks.[2] When we interact with those around us, we collect meaningful information. From observing the actions of others, we learn how to conduct ourselves and determine whether a person or situation is good for us or not. Ultimately, as we become adults, we've arrived at a set of patterns for interacting that shape how we develop our identity in relation to others, enjoy intimacy, work through and resolve conflict, learn to stand up for ourselves, cooperate, collaborate, and compromise—all of these social skills are enormously important for navigating the world and the people in it. These skills help us establish future romantic relationships and meaningful friendships, raise children, and build our careers and professional networks.

We know that staying connected to loved ones, fostering a rich social life, and nurturing empathy (i.e., the ability to understand at a deep level the perspectives and feel the emotions of another person) have a protective effect on our brain-body; they build our stress tolerance and buffer against bad anxiety. And when we learn how to hone these aspects of our social brain, we feel better and manage better in our lives. Indeed, good anxiety—the kind that comes from being emotionally regulated and attentive to all our emotions, including the negative, uncomfortable ones—can motivate us to be more outward-facing and interested in connecting with others. And yet, we also know that when we tip over into too much anxiety, when the stress or discomfort pushes us over a certain threshold, then our social confidence can break down.

According to several studies, chronic stress can disrupt brain cell functioning, which can make people lose a desire to be social and become avoidant of interactions with others. Chronic stress also has a "shrinking effect" on the prefrontal cortex, targeting memory functioning in particular. When we feel anxious, many of us withdraw or avoid social situations, which are coping strategies for dealing with the fear and discomfort, like a short-circuiting of our response to the anxiety: to avoid rather than deal with the trigger of the discomfort. So if we are wired to be social, then why do many of us get anxious at even the thought of putting ourselves out there? Why are joining a group outing, going to a party or event, or meeting new people such pain points for so many of us? Why is so much anxiety produced doing something we're literally born to do?

When this short-circuiting goes haywire and people develop a clinical level of social anxiety, doctors call it social anxiety disorder or SAD. There is a clear distinction between social anxiety disorder and the everyday anxiety any of us can experience when we feel nervous or even a bit fearful before or during a social event.

People who suffer from SAD have altered brain functioning in specific areas, including the anterior cingulate cortex (ACC),[3] and a kind of generalized hyperarousal of the limbic system. When it comes to everyday anxiety, we have the opportunity to channel arousal and focused attention toward what we are enjoying in any moment; this proactive shift can subdue an initial fearful response to certain social situations. If, for example, our initial response to feeling anxious about going to a party or joining an outing is to avoid it, we can learn to quell the fear. Furthermore, the more we build our social brain and its intelligence, the more we are able to buffer ourselves against social anxiety and the loneliness that can result.

Loneliness often goes hand in hand with bad anxiety, each making the other worse. It develops in part because of a lack of social attachment and interaction. Doctors and therapists often recommend engaging activities, reconnecting with family, friends, and colleagues, or a support group to treat loneliness. In other words, people are the cure to loneliness. But often the anxiety has become so intense and so unremitting that the brain actually changes as a result, creating abnormalities and errors in areas that affect how people perceive themselves in relation to others. Researchers call this *perceived loneliness*. (Some scientists have also theorized that these brain dysfunctions come first, like a kind of genetic abnormality that predisposes people to loneliness.) Regardless of this chicken-and-egg question, loneliness is harmful, exacerbates anxiety, and affects millions of people.[4]

A recent survey done by the health service company Cigna[5] using the UCLA Loneliness Scale reported that half of adult Americans today report feeling lonely. We now know that there are serious health risks associated with loneliness. For example, one meta-analysis that examined 300,000 patients showed that lonely people have a 50 percent greater probability of death compared to patients with adequate social relationships.[6] From a physiological perspective, higher levels of loneliness are associated with metabolic dysfunction, compromised immune system, disrupted sleep, higher incidence of cardiovascular disease, and higher rates of mortality.

So if bad social anxiety causes a cascade of problems and possibly gets in the way of us having the social relationships we need to thrive, how can good anxiety help us?

By understanding more about how the social brain works, and how we develop social intelligence, we can buffer against the negative effects of anxiety, including the fear response that might make us withdraw and become lonely. We can also use the arousal and piqued attention of good anxiety to help us connect with others in meaningful ways. Like strengthening a muscle group, we can strengthen our ability to empathize with people, and empathy is a kind of power to connect—the more we connect authentically with others, the healthier our overall brain-body systems and the richer our lives. And yet there's more: You can make empathy into a superpower—and that, my friends, is compassion.

· INSIDE THE SOCIAL BRAIN ·

The now famous story of one Phineas Gage[7] has led the study of modern-day understanding of the social brain. Gage, a railroad worker and later foreman in the mid-1800s, suffered an accident that permanently damaged his brain, specifically the part of the prefrontal cortex closest to the middle or "midline" of his brain. Before the accident he was described by those who knew him as a hardworking, responsible man who was "a great favorite" among the men who reported to him. But after his accident, the doctors who treated and studied Gage stated that though his general intelligence and most of his memory were unchanged, his personality and ability to interact with society completely changed. His employers were quoted as saying that after the accident, "the change in his mind [was] so marked that they could not give him his place again." Indeed, Gage was described as being "fitful, irreverent, and indulging in the grossest profanity (which was not previously his custom)." In fact, his friends and coworkers said, "Gage was no longer Gage." His whole personality had transformed.

The story of Phineas Gage is told in all neuroscience textbooks because it was our first clue to the essential role that the medial (i.e., toward the middle) part of the prefrontal cortex played in social intelligence. Since that famous case, other brain disorders have been discovered that also impair social interactions. Neuroscientists and cognitive psychologists refer to the key function impaired in Gage as *mentalization*, which refers to the ability to characterize our own and others' mental states appropriately. A familiar situation where mentalization is impaired is in autism, in which people have difficulties with social and verbal communication as well as with correctly characterizing the mental and emotional states of others (i.e., mentalizing).

Brain imaging studies have implicated two major areas in mentalizing. The first is smack dab in the middle of the area damaged in poor Mr. Gage, the medial part of the prefrontal cortex, which has previously been identified as the anterior cingulate cortex. This area is active when people monitor—or are aware of—their own mental states as well as the actions of others. Another brain area involved is the boundary region between the temporal and parietal lobes, called the temporoparietal junction. This region is active when subjects view others moving, and it may be most familiar to you as the general region where researchers in Italy found "mirror neurons."[8]

Mirror neurons function like the mentalization neurons in that they seem to activate during moments of empathy. While mirror neurons may not be the only key to understanding all aspects of empathy, growing evidence shows that their contribution to the brain areas involved in empathy is real.[9] The original discovery of mirror neurons was made in the early 1990s in macaque monkeys and showed that these unique neurons responded when the subject fed itself as well as when the subject saw someone else getting a treat.[10] More recent studies have identified a wider brain network involved in mirroring, including parts of the anterior insular cortex that are active during both directly experienced pain and empathetic pain (i.e., watching someone else endure pain).[11] While the social neuroscientific study of empathy has made great strides, the precise link between mirror neurons and empathy needs further study.[12]

Like so many other brain functions that we've discussed, empathy is generated both from bottom-up and top-down processes. It's reliant not only on the automatic functioning of the mirror neurons that pick up and recognize the emotions of others but also on the more conscious mentalizing capacity to infer the significance of how someone is feeling. A third component of empathy, however, is critical for our understanding here: self-awareness and emotion regulation. We need to feel grounded ourselves in order to take the perspective of another.

....

There are a very large number of brain areas that relate to social perception, including processing and reacting to social situations. Some of these areas are involved in decision making and focus, which affect how we interact socially, and are located in the PFC, while other social functions, such as how we process social situations (e.g., pick up social cues, read body language, etc.), seem to occur in the amygdala, where we also process our core emotional responses (see figure, next page). The key point to take away from this figure is the large number of brain areas we use and need to process and respond to social situations.

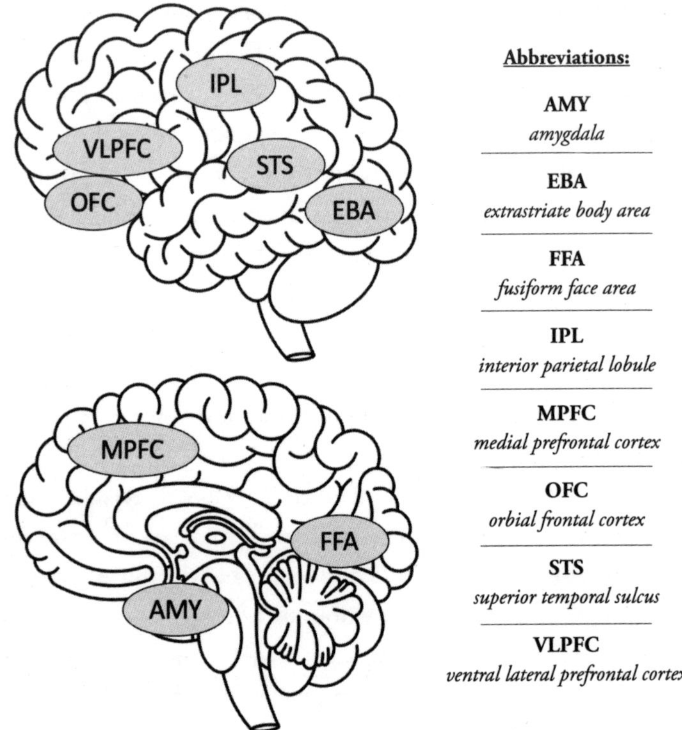

Figure 7. **The neuroanatomy of the social brain from Pelphrey and Carter**[13]

This figure and the anatomical investigations of the social brain suggest that social intelligence (SQ) is a blend of attention, perception, and emotion regulation. And as we've seen, all of these underlying neural networks affect how we manage our stress response and process anxiety.

· OXYTOCIN: THE LOVE HORMONE THAT BUFFERS ANXIETY ·

You have likely already heard of oxytocin. It is a darling of the popular press and has been touted as the "love hormone" and a surefire cure for shyness. You might have even googled "oxytocin" and found nasal sprays of this hormone in the most popular online marketplaces. But you might be surprised to learn of the wide range of functions oxytocin has in developing our social capacities (i.e., our social intelligence) and how its absence is linked to social anxiety disorder and loneliness.[14]

Oxytocin is made and released by brain cells in the hypothalamus, a small but crucial area in the middle of the brain. One of the most widely known functions of oxytocin occurs during childbirth. Not only does oxytocin stimulate uterine contractions, enabling the baby to make its way down the birth canal, the mother to deliver, and milk to be released from the breasts after birth, but it also fuels mother-child attachment. This is oxytocin's true power as a love hormone; without it, women have great difficulty bonding with their infants.

An exciting new part of the oxytocin story came to light after Professor Tom Insel,[15] the former director of the National Institute of Mental Health, and his colleagues discovered that oxytocin and a related neurohormone, vasopressin, controlled pair-bond formation in a cute little species called the *Microtus ochrogaster*, or prairie vole. In layman's terms, Professor Insel was able to identify oxytocin as the reason that prairie voles mate for life. Prairie voles are one of the handful of mammalian species that form essentially lifelong pair bonds. It turns out that to form this strong pair bond, females need oxytocin, which is released during the mating session, and the males need a related hormone called vasopressin. Since then other studies have shown how oxytocin enables us to learn the codes of social behavior and social recognition and to form meaningful bonds with others. Interestingly, each of these are qualities that are often missing in people suffering from chronic or long-term loneliness.

Oxytocin has been shown to "modulate" anxiety and help regulate the stress response by calming down the brain-body. For example, studies report that higher levels of oxytocin in the bloodstream result in a low stress response as well as lower anxiety response in depressed patients.[16] How does this work? One recent model suggests that the release of oxytocin elicits what scientists call *social coping*—asking for help or turning to others for support, which of course reduces anxiety.

Think about that for a minute: Our bodies are actually capable of producing a chemical that enables us to ask for help in order to feel less anxious and less lonely. Now think about what it might mean if that process gets interrupted or stymied.

Oxytocin is so important that there have been a wide number of efforts to find ways to artificially replace or stimulate it in humans. One you may have seen already is products meant to artificially increase levels of oxytocin intranasally in situations of anxiety to help stimulate that social coping behavior. In humans, scientists have examined the effects of intranasal application of oxytocin in both control subjects (adults with typical social relationships) and people with social anxiety disorder and those diagnosed with autism spectrum disorder (ASD). The results have been mixed and inconclusive. On the positive side, they have shown that intranasal oxytocin can decrease anxiety, improve social recognition, and increase social motivation. The bad news is that the results are highly variable and not always positive, in the sense that they do not reliably improve social mechanisms; they also vary across different populations. In fact, a recent review of these studies on the effects of intranasal oxytocin on anxiety/depression showed the results taken as a whole are too mixed to come to any clear conclusion.[17]

Is there still hope that we might be able to use intranasal oxytocin to help our response to anxiety? Yes. These studies are still in their early stages and there are still many interesting and viable manipulations left to try. In fact, any social neuroscientist will tell you that the work on oxytocin is growing every day, and while we might not know how to best use intranasal oxytocin to improve anxiety today, we are learning more and more about the mechanisms every day. Indeed, this research into oxytocin is inspiring: The more we understand its mechanisms and how we might increase its levels, the more we may be able to address social anxiety.

· THE POWER OF SQ ·

Empathy and its sister, compassion, are ultimately superpowers of anxiety. Understanding how we can build our capacity for both is based on the science of social intelligence, or SQ. One newer area of neuroscience research has focused on SQ and its importance to our overall sense of well-being. According to Daniel Goleman, thought leader and author of the bestselling books *Working with Emotional Intelligence*[18] and *Social Intelligence*,[19] there are five major functions of the social brain:

1) Interaction synchrony: This automatic coordination of nonverbal back-and-forth communication is learned initially between mother and infant, setting the stage for attachment, communication skills, and understanding how to expect and conduct regular interaction with others.

2) Types of empathy: Empathy is not just one thing. There's primal empathy, which enables us to automatically discern the obvious emotional states of others—fear, disgust, sadness, etc.—those wired-in emotions that don't take higher cognition to recognize or interpret; and then there's cognitive empathy, which is a learned skill requiring more nuanced and sophisticated inferences, recognition, attention, and perception. People who are socially sensitive or have a condition like autism can have difficulty empathizing or an inability to do so.

3) Social cognition: This is our general ability to manage ourselves in social groups, read facial expressions, listen, take turns conversing, and get along with others in a harmonious way.

4) Interaction or communication skills: These elementary skills enable us to talk, listen, and otherwise communicate with others.

5) Concern for others: This function is both rudimentary, enabling us to build bonds with others so that we get our basic needs met, and complex, helping us build deep, meaningful connections with others. In other words, we are born with the capacity to care for others because it serves us and our survival.

The pathways to develop these skills are hardwired in our brains; however, their healthy development relies on a number of factors. As I've mentioned, some of this wiring needs to be turned on early in life, when an infant is cared for, touched, looked at, and spoken to; this is the essence of healthy attachment.

· LAVON: LEVERAGING ANXIETY FOR SOCIAL GOOD ·

The good news is that our very plastic brain enables us to develop a lot of these social skills over time and through experience. Lavon grew up in a middle-class suburb outside Atlanta. He was neither the poorest nor the richest kid in school, but what his family of four may have lacked in their checking account, they made up for in love, support, and connection. Lavon's parents had always had a loving relationship. They were each other's best friend, they were never shy about PDA, and as two working parents they always supported each other's talents and ambitions along with a strong mutual desire to maximize family time. They showed this same unconditional love and support toward their two kids. As parents they tended to be on the strict side, but always emphasized their underlying love for each other. There were fights and disagreements and even raised voices, but also quick forgiveness, with their home filled much more of the time with the laughter of family and friends.

Lavon, two years older than his sister, was a nervous kid. He couldn't keep still, which sometimes aggravated his parents and got him into trouble at school. Then when he reached third grade he discovered basketball and started playing every day, hours on end. He not only got quite good but a lot of his "jitters" calmed down when he played. Clearly, the exercise and focus of competition helped calm his nervous system, addressing that first level of bad anxiety.

By the time he got to high school, Lavon was living for the game. He loved playing and being part of a team. He thrived on the positive team spirit, the camaraderie, and the shared love of the sport. Even when disagreements would occasionally flare up on the court, Lavon had a way of quickly defusing the situation. He was able to see the two sides of any situation, resist taking sides, and help divided factions compromise. He was the perfect team player and was soon looked to as a leader.

Lavon ended his high school career not winning the state championship despite a valiant effort, but still winning a basketball scholarship to a great college. Lavon had always been a good, though not a great, student. But soon after he arrived at college, the time required for almost daily basketball practice together with the new college-level workload left him struggling in his classes. Gradually, his confidence on the court was not enough to keep his anxiety at bay. His attention became fragmented, and he felt like he was always on edge. He became more distracted that his grades were subpar and distressed that perhaps he did not belong. He began to withdraw from his teammates, questioning whether playing ball was worth it.

Lavon knew he was struggling. But then something life-changing happened. He heard a little voice inside of him urging him to reach out for help, and he decided to listen. The first person he contacted was one of his coaches on the basketball team. Coach Phillips could not have been more supportive. He listened to Lavon's challenges, and realized that Lavon's penchant for perfectionism was holding him back from asking for the academic help he needed. The coach referred him to a tutor on campus who helped Lavon come up with more efficient study strategies that fit in with his intense basketball schedule.

Coach Phillips also knew how important it was for Lavon to feel like the valued member of the team that he truly was. He stayed in close contact to make sure Lavon was feeling better about being part of the team, even asking another player, Albert, to encourage Lavon to hang out. Lavon mentioned his struggle to Albert and discovered that Albert had gone through similar struggles when he was a freshman. Lavon realized that it was possible to work through the issues he was having and felt support at all levels to get it done.

Years after he finished college, Lavon often thought back on the value of the helping hands that supported him through that difficult time. He saw the power in reaching out for help and realized he wanted to help people in that way. He wanted to use his leadership and teamwork skills not only to help people but to do something good in the world. Lavon was learning how to maximize his social skills by building on his good anxiety.

During his senior year he went to work for the local congressional candidate, whom he had heard speak and in whose message he believed. Lavon soon became a huge asset in the upcoming election cycle and was a natural at the political life. He loved talking to people, sharing his stories and insights, and especially loved talking to people on the fence or those who held opposing views. He had a talent for open discussion with anyone with any view and enjoyed rather than shied away from it. He didn't need to "win" the conversation. This was empathy in action.

The takeaway from Lavon's story is twofold. First, Lavon had a lot of examples to look to of positive social interaction, watching his parents communicate with love and respect, and being part of a basketball team. He was then able to recognize in his own life the way these skills worked for him: They buffered his inherent "jitters," as he called them, and also became a vehicle for positive feedback from teammates and his coach, which helped reinforce his motivation to connect and persevere despite setbacks. Second, because he was able to see that these were actually tools at his disposal, he was also able to reach out and use them when he needed help. Asking for help, as any teacher will tell you, is not only a sign of a good student but also an indication of maturity and perseverance. Although at first glance this idea seems like common sense, it's actually a common misperception. Our culture (Western, American) is rooted in the concept of self-reliance and places enormous emphasis on being independent. Often these values of self-determination get confused with the idea that it's somehow bad to need help, as if asking for support is a sign of weakness. And yet what the science suggests is the exact opposite: Asking for help is a sign of strong social skills.

Lavon's anxiety was drawing his attention to his insecurities about his academic performance and to his insecurities about his role as a member of the basketball team. What is so important in this story is that Lavon recognized that his anxiety was not telling him he was a failure; it was telling him to ask for help. He was able to leverage his good anxiety to go beyond and develop his social confidence and empathy. He pushed it into this more expansive sense of empathy and found a way to be his most authentic self while also forging genuine connections with others.

· ADAM: YOU CAN LEARN SQ ·

Adam, an only child, was always shy and introverted. From the time he was a baby, he clung to his mother and cried if he could not see her in his line of sight. He got a little more adventurous as he got older but was always a quiet little boy with a soft voice who seemed socially awkward and anxious. His parents were quiet and reserved and didn't socialize much, so Adam had few opportunities from which to learn.

While Adam never had a lot of friends, he loved any kind of anime. He had a great imagination and got lost in the stories he created. He loved painting a picture with words, and it was no coincidence that the vast majority of the positive reinforcement he experienced in life came through his creations.

In high school and college, life for Adam consisted of writing his school papers, occasionally getting together with an acquaintance, but by and large he spent most of his time alone in front of a computer. After college, he got a job as a freelance software developer where he mainly worked by himself, as his job didn't require person-to-person contact, which seemed to fit him just fine. Every once in a while he would go on dates, but he just never felt like he knew what he was doing. He was also not sure any of the women would ever want a long-term relationship with him—wasn't he boring?

One day, through no fault of his own, he was let go from his job, which triggered an onslaught of worry about money, which then worsened because he had nobody to share his fears with. He knew if he told his parents they would overreact and that would just make him feel worse. He didn't want to be a burden to anyone. He soon found himself feeling intensely lonely for the first time in a long time. His writing, which had always been a source of comfort and pleasure, did not help. The feeling of loneliness scared him, but he didn't quite know what to do.

He had always craved more of a social life and network of friends, but he'd always felt too anxious and insecure to do anything about it. One of the best articles he read on the topic suggested that he start with building a social foundation based on something he already enjoyed, did well, and liked talking about. There was only one choice here: his own work. He imagined that he could talk about anime creation, the process, and his favorite artists. Then he came up with this idea: He was going to take a course in how to teach anime.

The class did wonders for Adam. Suddenly, every week he entered a space where he wanted to not only share and ask questions but interact and learn from the people there. Probably for the first time in his life he easily entered conversations with strangers, focused on all sorts of anime models. It was fun, it was easy, and he felt none of the anxiety he usually did starting a conversation with someone new.

He realized that all those tips for being more social really helped. There he was, taking a class with little or no fear of interacting with his fellow students and actually looking forward to the weekly class. But then, when he really hit his stride, he began to notice that one of the reasons he felt so comfortable was that a lot of the wannabe artists in his class were like him—quiet, shy, with a lot to say inside their heads but not a lot of practice speaking out loud. He realized he not only understood exactly where they were coming from but knew exactly what to do to help them along: just be patient and start small. He assumed the role of teacher, noticing that even a one-word answer was a great start; after class, he then tried to engage and encourage the other students in a conversation when it was easier to speak without as many people watching. Adam's biggest lesson was that empathy became the ultimate cure for his anxiety.

Did Adam suddenly become less of an introvert? No. Should he? No. But he learned that his anxiety about finding a place for himself in a social community could be alleviated by the same tools he used to cope with other anxieties. Storytelling and anime brought him joy and relief; by realizing that these interests could bring joy and relief to others, he found a way into a community. What's more, Adam's empathy allowed him to recognize that there were others struggling with the anxieties he knew all too well; by sharing his own coping strategies with them, his empathy became a lifeline to others who were struggling to find their own community, too. Everyone in his classes benefited from Adam's recognition that they shared common struggles and interests. He was simply more comfortable with his discomfort, and the vehicle for that was learning that empathy activated his social intelligence and gave him the confidence to change his interaction just enough. In that way, Adam's anxiety gave him access to a wonderful world of experiences he might not have had otherwise.

· THE SUPERPOWER OF COMPASSION ·

Empathy is amazing, but something else is even more amazing—compassion. Compassion is, in some sense, the most "simple" superpower of anxiety. In showing compassion for all of your personal anxiety triggers, you can actually lessen anxiety in others and yourself at the same time.

I think of compassion as empathy on steroids. Compassion begins with our awareness that our actions, thoughts, and words and ways of communicating with others have an effect, whether we see that effect or not. A simple gesture that may not last more than a couple of seconds has the power to bring someone else joy.

You don't have to do a twenty-four-hour marathon of compassionate gestures—it's okay to start small. Pay attention to where your anxiety is drawing your attention. Use those moments in your life as a starting point for reaching out to others. If you have anxiety as the new person at work, take the time to talk to the other new hires to make them feel at ease. If you struggle with balancing kids and work, take the time to give a word of encouragement to the other new mothers and fathers in your circle. Taking a moment to imagine what other people might be struggling with, possibly the same challenges or worries that you struggle with, can lead to an enormous sense of relief.

If you suffer from social angst, awkwardness, or dread, know that this is a perfectly normal response. No matter what it looks like, a lot of people are dealing with internal anxiety in social situations. But as you've seen, it is actually possible to build your social muscle and use it to boost your connections—and your anxiety is giving you clues to what icebreakers and lifelines other people might be grateful for you to extend. Truly listen to what your anxiety is signaling to you about where you feel uncertain or insecure, and practice empathy by offering a hand to others who might be in the same boat. Remember that flipping anxiety into compassion is something inherent in you—it is, in fact, what your anxiety was designed to do for you. Together, compassion and empathy can buffer against bad anxiety. You can use your anxiety to be more outward-facing. The outcome? The spread of compassion for your fellow human beings, other species, and the planet!

9

Boost Your Creativity

Creativity is often described as an innate talent that some of us have and most of us do not. It's described as mysterious, abstract, and unknowable—which is why we find it so provocative. In the early part of my life, the concept of creativity made me imagine the stunning paintings of Picasso or Cézanne, the richness of Virginia Woolf's prose, the mind-blowing breadth of Frank Gehry's Guggenheim Museum Bilbao, or the transcendent Renaissance cathedrals of Europe. In science, the creative genius of scientists like Marie Curie, Einstein, or, more recently, Mary-Claire King (discoverer of the breast cancer gene) moved me. The music of Joni Mitchell, Bach, Lady Gaga, and James Taylor inspired me. Yes, creativity seemed to be the realm of artists and geniuses. But like many people, I had gotten it all wrong. The modern conception of creativity shows that it's a fundamental capacity of the human brain, something not only transportive, like an artistic masterpiece, but also quite ordinary. Creativity is what we exercise when we solve a puzzle or problem, when we come up with a new way to knit a sweater or pile logs in the yard. Creativity is comprised of problem solving, invention, insight, and innovation. It's big and small and always innately human and deeply enriching.

Just as bad anxiety can tip us into a mindset that harms our performance rather than helps it, we know that bad anxiety can shut down creativity. A classic example would be writer's block. But is anxiety literally blocking the neural pathways to thinking in a creative way, or does the physical state of anxiety freeze our thinking in any way, creative or otherwise? What's often misunderstood is how anxiety can actually sometimes *fuel* creativity, giving people the fodder to delve deep into themselves and come out the other side; creativity can give us a way to process our negative feelings, including anxiety. Once again, anxiety offers us a way to reframe our understanding of creativity, and with this understanding we create (no pun intended) new ways of dealing with anxiety.

· MICHAELA: HOW ANXIETY CAN SQUELCH CREATIVITY ·

Michaela was always on a deadline. As a freelance editor and writer, she was a constant worker bee, always juggling more writing projects than she could handle. She would justify her hyperstress mode as a simple fact of life, and she believed that living on the edge was part of the freelancer lifestyle. She worried constantly about being able to pay her bills, never mind put money away for a rainy day.

Living in this way was taking its toll. She had recently been diagnosed with Hashimoto's disease, an autoimmune disorder that impacts the thyroid. Some of the effects of the thyroid not functioning well are fatigue, irritability, and anxiety. For the past few months, the only way she managed to get her work done was by taking a midday nap and going to bed by 8:30 p.m. And yet despite the naps, the quality of her work was just not at her typical high level; her projects were completed on time but they lacked luster. She broke up with a boyfriend, feeling that any relationship was more than she could handle, and she kept her social dates to a minimum. Her life had been reduced to all work and no play.

Michaela's doctor put her on thyroid medicine and then told her in no uncertain terms that if she didn't get a hold of her chronic stress, she could expect other conditions to crop up as well. This threat got Michaela's attention. She realized that she needed to make some immediate changes to her lifestyle, so she cleaned up her diet and added exercise and meditation. At the suggestion of a nutritionist, she also started taking a supplement called gamma-aminobutyric acid (GABA), which has been shown to improve mood and lessen anxiety, and began to research more about how Hashimoto's gets triggered by stress. She learned how chronic stress depletes the brain-body system in numerous ways: When the adrenal glands release too much cortisol, significant brain areas are negatively affected, including the hippocampus, the amygdala, and the PFC. The body is also impacted by chronic high cortisol through an increased likelihood of high blood pressure, diabetes, and heart disease, along with an increased vulnerability to autoimmune disorders.

When I met her, we talked about how she was dealing with stress. For Michaela, taking charge of her stress response meant a kind of leaning into her anxiety, not away from it. This information got Michaela thinking about what was truly important to her: Did she want to be a freelancer forever? Did she need the freedom to create her own schedule, or would she feel more grounded with a stable job that came with a salary? She had always thought she needed the freelance lifestyle in order to be creative and productive. But now she was having second thoughts: Her constant worry about money and finding her next gig was clearly part of her chronic stress. Maybe some financial stability would decrease her anxiety? Following the threads of her anxiety back to her conflicting emotions about freelance work versus a steady income gave her valuable insight into other lifestyle changes that she could consider in order to make a big change.

Michaela began to reframe her thinking and applied for a couple of positions for in-house writers. The content was not that exciting to her personally—it was a magazine devoted to dogs and cats—but it paid well. She would have a predictable schedule and benefits, so she could feel a stronger sense of security. She decided to give it a try. Within a month, she felt much less anxious. In fact, she felt more energetic, in part because of the medicine, but also because her life felt more balanced. She discovered that she had extra energy that she began to pour into her personal writing projects. She began by simply writing in a journal every morning like clockwork. She'd read Julia Cameron's *The Artist's Way* and started with journaling for just three pages, with no specific agenda. Then the three pages grew to five and then six. Soon, the outline of a novel took shape.

Michaela's worries about money had fueled her high anxiety, preventing her from being able to pursue her creative ambitions of writing a novel and even resulting in an actual disease. But she was not really motivated to make positive changes until her anxiety made itself impossible to ignore. But when she took a step back and looked closely at her life and habits, she realized that she did not want to accept a life curtailed by anxiety and now an autoimmune disease. She had ignored her anxiety about money for so long that it had converted into a more attention-getting health crisis. Only then was she able to appreciate what her anxiety was telling her—she needed to reexamine the story she was telling herself and make some changes. Taking a full-time job meant doing something that was outside the story she had been telling—but it also gave her a life that was much closer to the one she wanted.

Ultimately, Michaela was able to repurpose her energy in a creative, meaningful way. And here is the best part: She had always separated her own writing from writing that paid, but with her renewed energy she discovered that this false separation had only been fueling her anxiety. She also realized an additional benefit, one that seemed to be life-changing for her: that with her anxiety under control, she now had the mental and emotional space and the physical energy to be more creatively productive. And that was the best gift of all.

Michaela's story not only illustrates our ability to change our behaviors but also highlights the power of creativity as a source of transformation and healing. Michaela will always have to deal with her thyroid disorder; she will always have to be careful of her body's overzealous stress response. However, now that she knows how to manage her stress response and can control her anxiety, her creativity has become a source of energy, balance, and well-being.

· ARE THERE CREATIVITY TRAITS? ·

I guess you could say that I've had to acknowledge or admit that I am, indeed, creative. A few years ago I never would have given myself that designation. But the research and my own experience have proved me wrong. We can all be creative. At the same time, it's interesting to keep in mind how researchers have qualified the traits of creative people, as if there are definable personality or temperament traits associated with creativity.

According to studies, creative people show:

- a tolerance for ambiguity
- perseverance
- relative disinterest in social approval
- an openness to experience (i.e., new experiences)
- a pro-risk attitude

Some people are indeed born with these temperament traits but others, myself included, would check off less than half of the list. Does thinking creatively depend on all of these? Or a few?

My point here is that one of the many misconceptions about creativity is the idea that you need to have a creative personality in order to be creative, think creatively, or use creative thinking as a vehicle to problem-solve or innovate. But understanding that the types of thinking that enable creativity can be learned, consider each of these traits and the likelihood that you can choose to:

- tolerate ambiguity: Isn't this similar to becoming more comfortable with difficult or painful emotions, such as anxiety?
- persevere in the face of obstacles or failures: Isn't this nurturing an activist mindset and choosing to plow on, using feedback to try again?
- disregard the potential for social disapproval: Isn't this a willingness to think for yourself and ask for help when you need it?
- adopt an open attitude toward new experiences or a change in behavior: Isn't this the essence of cognitive flexibility?
- get out of your comfort zone and try something without a guarantee of success: Isn't this a desire to engage, learn, and enjoy an activity for the heck of it?

Why do I think adopting a creative approach to life is beneficial? Because it reinforces flexibility, openness, and a yearning to learn and grow. And all of us have the potential to be creative and use that creativity to control the negative aspects of anxiety and channel what's good. It comes down to developing the skills that come with good anxiety: an activist mindset, a willingness to train your attention on a specific goal, and the courage to try. It's also a reminder of the importance of learning how to tolerate these negative states not JUST for creativity but for helping to transform your anxiety into a superpower. For me, for a very long time I could not tolerate a lot of disapproval. I always sought approval and support before moving forward, which kept me on a positive and productive path in science in some ways, but likely blocked me from even more creative discoveries in others. For me, I had to get to that level of seniority where others sought my approval for me to realize that whoever happened to have seniority at the moment was not necessarily the best guide—maybe it was the newest person on the team who had the really creative idea to share. That really helped me get over my attachment to social approval. Failures taught me how to improve my work; even those negative comments I got on the first iterations of a new product were so helpful in quickly pushing me away from a bad track to a better one. Failure is part of the process; feedback helps us improve. Not that I seek out those negative views, but they help you hone your ideas or products like no rave review will ever do!

· SO WHAT IS CREATIVITY? ·

One of the best definitions I have come across is this: Creativity is "the ability to produce work that is both novel (i.e., original, unexpected) and appropriate (i.e., useful, adaptive concerning task constraints)."[1] While we are still relatively early in our scientific study of creativity, we are gradually coming to a consensus about some of the underlying neural pathways and processes that are engaged during any kind of creative exercise. Before we look inside the brain, so to speak, let's further define creativity.

As one scientist says,[2] creativity is "essentially a Darwinian process" because it always comes down to selecting which new ideas are also appropriate, relevant, or useful. Is Einstein's theory of relativity novel? Check! Is it useful? Double check! Is an out-of-work fashion designer's discovery that she can use her "free" time during COVID to make face masks instead of fancy T-shirts and scarves novel? Check! Is it useful? Check again. Creativity inspired scientists to harness the power of T cells and turn them into cancer-cell killers, and creativity led to the fusion of hip-hop and American history to create the phenomenon of *Hamilton*. Allowing our minds to wander outside of what is familiar stimulates creativity.

From a neuroscience point of view, creativity is a form of *information processing* that can be emotional or cognitive, deliberate or spontaneous:

- spontaneous experience of insight or epiphany when the solution to a problem appears
- after much persistence and hard work (e.g., deliberation) you gain a new understanding or make a new connection

We can recognize how creativity shows up in real life. The anthropologist working in the field for three years interviewing subjects and reviewing long research articles may not consider the long days and nights, the arduous yet somewhat mechanical task of taking notes and transcribing them from audio into written form, a creative process. But when she sits down and begins to synthesize the notes, pulling out the overarching themes that occur in the varied interviews, this process of mulling and drawing connections and conclusions is a creative process. The slog, the persistence, and the research are all part of what enables the connections and insight to occur.

My dear friend, creativity expert, and author of *Spark: How Creativity Works*[3] Julie Burstein agrees that creativity is not a capacity of a few but an ability that we can all grow and nurture. She says that we can all activate this capacity if we:

- pay attention to the world around us and remain open to new ways of thinking and being
- embrace challenge and adversity and learn how to push up against our perceived limits
- let go enough to play around
- know that our most difficult emotional experiences that inevitably come with human existence can fuel our creative expression

Note that half of these suggestions about how to enhance creativity focus on challenge or difficult emotional experiences while the other half (i.e., enhanced attention and letting go) require feeling relaxed enough and not held back by too much stimulation or arousal: Essentially, being in the good-anxiety band of cognitive function. Interestingly, even bad anxiety can lead to something different. Our inevitable struggles, stress, pain, fear, and discomfort often become motivation to seek relief, some sort of solution or answer to why we are feeling bad. These negative feelings can be valuable raw materials for creative insights or creations. The superpowers of mindset, productivity, and performance require a shift from bad to good anxiety in order to work. What we are starting to understand about the superpower of creativity is that at least part of it is accessed and inspired by one's struggles with painful emotions.

There is much disagreement among scientists and theorists about how to study creativity and how to trace its processes to functional pathways or structural areas. Indeed, as two of the major creativity experts say in their recent overview on creative thought, "There is not a single cognitive or neural mechanism we can rely on to explain the extraordinary creative capacities of an Einstein or a Shakespeare."[4]

My point? Creativity is special—and in many ways. And creativity is a product of our efforts to process our emotions. So let's first look at what we know about the brain basis of creativity and then explore how we can leverage our good and bad anxiety to up our capacity to be fully and life-expandingly creative.

· WHERE CREATIVITY SHOWS UP IN THE BRAIN ·

Though at first neuroscientists thought of the PFC as the "seat" of creativity, we now know that many areas of the brain are involved in creative thinking: abstract thinking, self-reflection, cognitive flexibility, mentalizing and empathy, working memory, and sustained and directed attention. These discrete ways of processing cognition and emotion overlap and interact in different creative tasks.[5]

Any left-handed person knows the old joke "If the right side of the brain controls the left side of the body, then only lefties are in their right minds." The right side of the brain (referring to the right hemisphere) has long been associated with passion, emotion, and illogic. And we also know that it's the left side where language and analytical, logical, and practical thought are located. Well, you might be surprised to learn creativity is not housed in either the right side or the left side. The most recent research on the neural basis of creativity shows that a widespread network of brain areas is involved in the process of creativity. For example, while the creative spark—aka an "aha" moment—seems to occur in one specific brain area, the anterior superior temporal gyrus in the temporal lobe on the right side of the brain, many more brain areas are involved in the creative process.[6]

Neuroscientists have identified three major brain networks that *generate* creativity. You are already familiar with one of these, the executive control network, known for recruiting and organizing our focus and attention. The other two—the salience network and the default mode network—also help to map out the many interactions between top-down and bottom-up processing that involve different dimensions of creative thinking.

The Executive Control Network. The executive control network, which you learned about in the chapter on attention, is centralized in the prefrontal cortex and manages inhibitory control and working memory. Both are necessary for recruiting and maintaining focus and also play an important role in the creative process. Another key function of the prefrontal cortex—cognitive flexibility—is also at the heart of creativity. This part of the executive function is what enables us to look at a problem in a new way, try new strategies that lead to new solutions, and enable breakthroughs in thinking. Cognitive flexibility is necessary for approaching problem solving creatively.

The Salience Network. The second brain network that relates to creativity is called the salience network. This is a broad network of brain structures that monitors both external events and internal thoughts and allows the brain to shift between the two, depending on the task at hand. Areas involved in this network include the dorsal anterior cingulate cortex, housed within the prefrontal cortex, as well as the anterior insular cortex. It also includes the amygdala, the ventral striatum, the dorsomedial thalamus, the hypothalamus, and parts of the striatum. Creative thinking is marked by an ability to think flexibly and switch back and forth between ideas, feelings, external stimuli, memories, and imagination. When the salience network is stimulated by good anxiety, it allows fast switching between what can be thought of as the internal and external sources of creative inspiration.

The Default Mode Network (also known as the Imagination Network). The third network involved in creativity is the default mode network (DMN). This area of the brain has historically been associated with mind-wandering. It's when our brains are at rest and not focused on a deliberate task that the brain's default mode network kicks in and is allowed to roam. This network is a good example of how anxiety can be good or bad. When the DMN is stuck in perseveration or rumination, it worsens anxiety; but when you are aware of the DMN and use it as a way to brainstorm, then anxiety is positive and can be fodder for creativity and imagination. Indeed, recent research has shown that the brains of highly creative people demonstrate a poorer capacity for attention than their less creative counterparts.[7] When studied using fMRI, this state is marked by distinct but diffuse patterns of activity across many pathways. Though scientists refer to this state as one of "rest," it's only a rest or break from deliberate or effortful attention and focus. In other words, activation of the DMN means a lot of thinking and connections are being made subconsciously. Neuroscientist Randy Buckner describes the DMN as being involved in "constructing dynamic mental simulations based on personal past experiences such as used during remembering, thinking about the future, and generally when imagining alternative perspectives and scenarios to the present."[8] For that reason, another thought leader in the area of human creativity, Scott Barry Kaufman, likes to call the DMN the "imagination network." This network also involves areas within the prefrontal cortex, the medial temporal lobe—including the hippocampus, critical for long-term memory—as well as the parietal lobe.

The importance of these three networks was recently confirmed by a study[9] showing a person's capacity to generate original ideas can be reliably predicted from the strength of the connections within and among these networks.

· DECONSTRUCTING CREATIVITY ·

In the spirit of the clean, well-defined, focused, and scientific approach to creativity, two major processing modes of creativity have been identified: spontaneous and deliberate. Spontaneous creativity refers to those seemingly unexplained "aha" moments of insight that emerge out of nowhere and has always been associated with the DMN. Deliberate creativity, on the other hand, is a top-down process that is strategic, effortful, and oriented around problem solving, which is why it involves the executive control network as well as the salience network.

In a popular story in both psychology and chemistry, in 1890 the famous German chemist Friedrich August Kekulé described a dream he had while dozing in front of a fire of a snake "self-devouring" that led him to the idea of the circular nature of the chemical benzene, or benzene ring. This story has often been held up as a demonstration of spontaneous creativity. However, more recent analysis suggests that others had already discovered and illustrated benzene as a ring-shaped structure at the time and the dream story was a creative way not to have to share the credit for that discovery. While the first example involves spontaneous creativity, the latter interpretation is clearly an example of deliberate creativity.

Is there a benefit to forming hard lines in the sand, distinguishing the two types of creative thinking? I say yes. Just as with creating an environment where flow could occur, you have to do the work to both anticipate and experience the release and engagement of being in the creativity zone. Yes, the spark of insight or invention might feel effortless, but it's always preceded by some kind of preparation.

Creativity allows for—even encourages—us to become comfortable with all of our feelings, including anxiety. Further, anxiety does an excellent job of drawing our attention to the things that are likely to provoke an emotional response—an essential part of creating. Emotional energy—whether in the form of negative or positive feelings—can often be the *inspiration* for creative work, such as art, writing, and music. But the *production* of that work pulls on cognition as well. The interactivity of the three networks, and the practical distinction between spontaneous and deliberate, emotional and cognitive, raises an important point about creativity: Regardless of how spontaneous or effortful a creative insight may be, the brain always draws on knowledge that is stored in our emotional and cognitive memory banks. As neuroscientist Arne Dietrich says, "in art as well as science, the expression of a creative insight requires a high level of skill, knowledge, and/or technique that depends upon continuous problem solving."[10] Creativity connects the emotional and cognitive processes that help us become more comfortable with our anxiety; what's more, the creative process can actually be a release valve for that anxiety as we practice converting it into something beautiful.

This explains why some scientists have suggested that there are five stages to the creative process:[11]

1) preparation with immersion in task or curiosity about topic or subject area
2) incubation
3) generation of solutions or assembling pieces of a puzzle
4) generation of criteria to evaluate
5) selection and decision making and/or implementation

As you consider honing your own creative spirit, think about how the arousal, awareness, and engagement of your good anxiety can help you not dwell on or accept frustration if you're trying to solve a problem, stimulate your curiosity, or inspire you to get out of your comfort zone and try something new.

· USING CREATIVE THINKING TO EMBRACE ANXIETY ·

At one level the same processes that enable creative thinking are what enable the shift from bad to good anxiety:

- It is cognitive flexibility that enables us to reframe a situation and lessen our physiological stress response.
- It is the ability to put ourselves in someone else's point of view that enables us to come up with another way to perceive our threat response.
- It is sustained and directed attention that enables us to increase our understanding of our anxiety and then exert more top-down control over how we act on it.

Creative thinking not only reinforces our tools to make the shift from bad to good anxiety, but also emerges when you're in a good anxiety state. For instance, the brains of creative people show a reduced ability to filter out extraneous information; in other words, creative people are less able to stay narrowly focused.[12] The implication? That creative thinkers are expansive and holistic in their thinking.

Experiments that look specifically at how to train the capacity for divergent thinking has been shown to "teach" the brain to be more creative.[13] I learned this firsthand. As a career scientist I have a list of creative insights from throughout the years that I'm very proud of. Some are practical, some esoteric (e.g., only if you have been studying the electrophysiology of the hippocampus for many years would you understand why a particular insight was, in fact, quite creative). But perhaps the insight I'm most proud of was born out of an intense, hit-the-wall problem I needed to solve.

....

My own example of creativity born from anxiety is actually one of the things I'm most proud of from my graduate neuroscience research. The first thing to know is that I spent six years getting my PhD. I was studying the brain areas important for memory that sit next to the hippocampus, and the work I was doing was very exciting, but also long and tedious. Half my task was mapping out the connections of these areas that sit next to the hippocampus; before these studies, we had no idea how they connected to the rest of the brain. I knew the experiments we were doing had the potential to be really groundbreaking—we were exploring a brain area that had fallen through the cracks of neuroscience research, and we suspected that it carried the key to our understanding of how long-term memory works in the brain. But I also knew that if I didn't have good tools to display my anatomical findings, I would never really know in detail the findings I was sitting on. What to do!

The studies that I did helped show that these previously unappreciated brain areas were not only strongly interconnected with the hippocampus but also received widespread input from all over the brain and acted as a kind of funnel area that gathered the widespread information and processed it for the hippocampus. To do these anatomical studies I put small discrete injections of special dyes in these brain areas I was focused on, and that dye ended up being transported to the cell bodies of all the other cells that connected to that brain area that was injected. I spent hundreds of hours throughout my graduate career manually looking for those labeled individual brain cells, and using a computer system to note their location on an outline I could draw the thin slice of brain I was studying. Because the areas I was studying received projections from widespread areas throughout the brain, it meant I had hundreds of thin slices per brain to painstakingly scan and plot out on, one by one, the labeled cells I saw.

That part took a lot of time, but we had the equipment and good microscopes to do it just fine. I knew that the potential significance of my findings would hinge on how well I was able to convey the impact of these projections I was seeing and what it meant for the functions of these brain areas. Studies done before mine had adopted a very imprecise way of showing the brain areas and the labeled cells by doing general sketches of the surface of the brain with "artistic rendering" of the approximate distribution of the labeling. But these illustrations lacked the detail about the distinct cell layers and the beautiful broad brain–labeling patterns that differed between cases. There was a more precise way to show the data, which was more promising. That was creating what is known as a two-dimensional unfolded map of the brain. But it was 100 percent manual and there was no way to automate it. Without extra help, I felt like I was looking at an eight- or nine-year graduate career to manually analyze all my data in this way, which is why previous scientists had opted for the more artistic but qualitative whole-brain rendering I described above.

Did this cause me worry and anxiety? It sure did! Graduate school was one six-year stint of getting used to the ambiguity of scientific research. I knew I was working with world-class scientists, but that did not guarantee me a world-class finding to focus my doctoral dissertation on.

I was caught between a rock and a hard place with years of "manual" labor looming before me. I did the only thing I could do in this situation: I had to get creative in order to "solve" this problem. For weeks, I was just turning over in my mind how I could modify the method or automate it in some way that had not been done before. It was almost as though I could feel my executive control, salience, and imagination networks passing the idea back and forth. I was a stressed-out graduate student worried that my thousands of hours of microscope work would not amount to the important scientific breakthrough I thought it should be.

One day I was puzzling over what to do, feeling increasingly anxious. I began manually lining up my unfolded brain sections one by one and that's when the idea came to me. These lined-up brain sections looked like the rows in the Excel spreadsheet I had just been working on a few minutes before. In fact, as I flattened out the section and subdivided the cortex into little chunks, I could count the labeled cells in each little chunk of cortex. It started to look even more like the rows and columns of an Excel spreadsheet! I kind of knew how Excel worked at that point but hadn't really used it very much. But I felt like that spark of an idea was worth fanning. It was right before holiday break so I flew home to San Jose, California, with the Excel manual in my bag so I could study the Excel spreadsheet over the break and see if I could somehow use it to help automate my anatomical analysis. It turned out that not only were the rows and columns of Excel exactly analogous to the way I had been creating my unfolded maps of the brain manually, but I could use its programming language to create a little macro to color-code the different cells depending on how many labeled cells were found in that chunk of the cortex. Chunks with one hundred cells could automatically be colored red, while the chunks with only ten could automatically be colored gray.

I leaped for joy in my parents' living room that Christmas as I pored over that manual. While I had not discovered a fully automated system, it gave me a new quantitative way to illustrate and store the data from all my experiments, and I ended up using my Excel spreadsheet brain analysis hack for years to come as did the other members of the lab. This was a feat of creativity inspired and pushed by bad anxiety. But I also know that the stress of the moment was the light that fired me up to find my solution. I now see the problem solving I did in this project as a clear example of divergent thinking blended with cognitive flexibility and sustained attention.

....

Creativity is a skill that needs to be practiced; it also asks that you "follow" it, often going outside your comfort zone. My biggest challenge to get out of my comfort zone and do something that does not guarantee success? I have two words for you: cabaret singing. I took a cabaret singing workshop in New York in which the final meant I had to sing two songs solo onstage with a band backing me. YIKES! There were some beautiful singers in that class and some okay ones. I was squarely in the latter category. I loved all the practice sessions and the one-on-one session I had with the instructor, but the night of the performance was terrifying! I sang "Walkin' My Baby Back Home," the Nat King Cole version, and "Sway," the Michael Bublé version—both songs I love. I won no Grammys that night, but I'll always remember the woman sitting in the front row on the left who was smiling and tapping her foot the whole way through my songs. That might have been one of the bravest things I've ever done. I had opened up another creative outlet that I am still exploring, and I'm still singing.

· CREATIVITY AND THE TRAGIC GAP ·

Julie Burstein's *Spark: How Creativity Works*[14] helped me understand creativity in a much more nuanced way. In her wonderful book, Julie describes the story of the writer Richard Ford, who grew up with dyslexia that left him able to read only very slowly. But what Ford realized after many years is that the requirement that he read very slowly allowed him to appreciate the rhythm and cadence of the language in a much deeper way. In fact, he attributes this attention to the detail of language to what made him the Pulitzer Prize–winning writer he is today.

I just love this story because it shows so beautifully how something that is so acutely associated with pain, frustration, and anxiety (i.e., lifelong dyslexia) can, when in the right mindset, actually fuel creativity.

This relationship between deep psychological or emotional pain and creativity is not new. Some artists have suffered deeply from anxiety and depression. Think of the artists—Van Gogh, Anne Sexton, Michelangelo, Georgia O'Keeffe, for example—who have been known to suffer emotional distress, and others who, in some cases, ended up taking their own lives. Although I don't think pain is a prerequisite to be a successful artist, the associations are worth contemplating.

Julie says that one way into creativity is through pain. She likens this capacity to generating positive energy, growth, and insight from grief. She sees the pool of negative emotions that define depression and anxiety as an opportunity to experience the full range of these difficult feelings, the dark, painful, negative ones as well as the fun, playful, joyous ones. By embracing grief and loss, Julie suggests, we can encounter what the educator Parker Palmer calls the "tragic gap," that gap between what exists in the world and what you want to create; it's like staring the void of space in the face and being brave enough to say, "I'll give it a go!"

I see an additional interpretation of the tragic gap: the gap that gets triggered by bad anxiety and points to our innate desire to create.

It's from Julie that I learned what neuroscientists are in the process of discovering: that creativity is about the tension between what you can control and what you let go; it's about being effortful and effortless; it's about embodying the push and pull between bad and good anxiety; it's about harnessing the arousal, activation, and engagement of anxiety while resisting the overexertion that comes from too much worry, perseveration, and overthinking of our endless what-ifs. Creativity, understanding the dimensions of its processes (for it's not just one process), will not only positively activate your capacity for creative expression but also open you up to using more of your brain than you ever thought possible.

We can use pain to help us create something new, useful, life-altering, and meaningful. It's up to you. But the process itself is one that is ultimately cathartic, taking us outside ourselves and giving something back to the world.

PART THREE

The Art of Worrying Well: Tools to Calm, Flip, and Channel Your Anxiety

So how do we begin to utilize and maximize this wondrous plasticity of our brains? How do we give ourselves the opportunity to make other choices, choices that are more positive for us? How can we do a better job of managing our anxiety and learning to channel it?

Throughout this book, you've been learning about how the brain works and the underlying networks and interactions that occur when we experience anxiety and try to avoid it. And I hope you've gained some appreciation for how scientists have been studying the brain, its interactions, and what we can do to harness our own emotions, reactions, and behaviors to better serve us. All the chapters in Part Two show how the varying pathways that anxiety travels can be accessed and utilized to accelerate our focus, improve our performance, enhance our creativity, and up our social IQ. And when we get better at all of these, we not only support our resilience and better manage our anxiety but also open the door to superpowers.

So now it's time to turn the focus to you.

You may find that some of the superpowers of anxiety come to you more easily than others. For example, you may find you're more drawn to utilizing anxiety's attention pathway to up your productivity because right now you really need to meet that deadline. Or you may be interested in how anxiety's arousal can help you improve your performance, even getting a taste of turning on flow. You may realize that one of the reasons you've been feeling so anxious and out of sorts lately is that you've spent way too much time in isolation; it's time to reach out and reconnect with friends and family.

All of anxiety's pathways will help you manage anxiety; and they can also lead to hidden superpowers. But first things first. In the following pages I've assembled some questionnaires and surveys that can guide your awareness of your own experience of anxiety right now. The questionnaires are meant to help you zero in on how you experience anxiety, what situations typically trigger it, and how you usually cope with it. Inherent in this process of self-reflection is the first step of not only quieting your anxiety so that it doesn't get in your way but also activating the mindset that enables you to flip it. Although we've been talking about flipping your anxiety from bad to good, it's more accurate to think of this process as shifting your orientation toward your anxiety. Pay attention to the information your anxiety is suggesting. Once you gain this objectivity, then you can reappraise a situation, thoughts, or memories. With this pivot you are then in a position to make a conscious decision about what to do with the feelings.

This awareness is key to helping you manage anxiety, lessen its impact, or, if you wish, begin to channel it.

The triggers for anxiety are ubiquitous and never-ending, but our responses to these stressors do not have to be inevitable. We do have the capacity to "optimize" our response to them. The idea here is that I want you to be able to take full advantage of the major goal of anxiety—a warning sign to protect against possible danger—and direct its stimulation of your brain-body.

As you become more aware of the common triggers that make you anxious, you can decide instead of simply avoiding these triggers to choose the course that is right for you.

These exercises are designed to be practical, concise, and doable. You should be able to easily pick whichever tools appeal to you and start exploring their effectiveness in your life today. The goal is to use these tools to begin to manage your anxiety so that it doesn't interfere in your life and then learn ways to utilize its energy. Ultimately, these techniques will help you make anxiety your friend. It's essential that you befriend your anxiety and know it like an old schoolmate. Familiarity will allow you to develop your arsenal of tools to modulate, minimize, and shift your bad anxiety to good, and will allow you to not only carefully monitor your progress—both successes and failures—but celebrate all successes, big and small.

· GET TO KNOW YOUR ANXIETY ·

How you experience anxiety on any given day changes. For now, and as a way to become more aware of how you respond to and process anxiety, answer the following set of questions. Keep in mind, your answers today may be different from tomorrow's or next week's. This is never an indictment of you. Your responses are information for you to use.

Try to be honest with yourself as you answer these questions, and pay attention to the subtleties and nuances of your emotional experience. Understanding how to recognize where you are on this continuum at any given time helps identify your personal anxiety baseline.

SURVEY #1:
HOW ANXIOUS ARE YOU?

The following list of questions will help you evaluate how anxious you are feeling right now. I encourage you to respond to these questions whenever it occurs to you, as your experience of anxiety is so dynamic. The answer you choose (1, 2, 3, 4) is your score on that question. Add up your scores to all the questions to calculate your baseline anxiety score.

A. How often over the last few weeks have you been bothered by feeling nervous or worried?

1. Not at all
2. Several days
3. More than half the days
4. Nearly every day

SCORE: ______

B. How often over the last few weeks have you had trouble relaxing or enjoying yourself?

1. Not at all
2. Several days
3. More than half the days
4. Nearly every day

SCORE: ______

C. How often over the past few weeks have you become easily irritated or annoyed by a situation or someone else?

1. Not at all
2. Several days
3. More than half the days
4. Nearly every day

SCORE: ______

D. ***How often over the last few weeks have you felt afraid, as if something awful might happen?***

1. Not at all
2. Several days
3. More than half the days
4. Nearly every day

SCORE: ______

E. ***How often in the last few weeks have you had trouble sleeping or experienced a change in your sleeping schedule?***

1. Not at all
2. Several days
3. More than half the days
4. Nearly every day

SCORE: ______

F. ***How often over the past few weeks have you overeaten or binged on a favorite edible treat?***

1. Not at all
2. Several days
3. More than half the days
4. Nearly every day

SCORE: ______

G. ***How often in the past few weeks have you had trouble concentrating or maintaining focus?***

1. Not at all
2. Several days
3. More than half the days
4. Nearly every day

SCORE: ______

H. ***How often over the past few weeks have you coped with your anxiety by turning to substances such as alcohol, marijuana, pain medicine, or others to dull your feelings?***

1. Not at all
2. Several days
3. More than half the days
4. Nearly every day

SCORE: ______

I. ***How often over the past few weeks have you been late for work, school, or other appointments?***

1. Not at all
2. Several days
3. More than half the days
4. Nearly every day

SCORE: ______

J. ***How often over the past few weeks have you declined an invitation to spend time with friends or family?***

1. Not at all
2. Several days
3. More than half the days
4. Nearly every day

SCORE: ______

K. ***Over the past few weeks how consistent has your physical activity been (including walking)?***

1. I have exercised regularly over this time frame.
2. I've just missed a handful of days of regular exercise over this time frame.

3. I've missed more than half my usual opportunities to move my body over this time frame.
4. I've not exercised at all during this time frame.

SCORE: ______

L. ***On a scale from 1 to 10 with 1 being the lowest and 10 being off the scales, how would you rate your level of overall anxiety over the past few weeks?***

1 2 3 4 5 6 7 8 9 10

SCORE: ______

TOTAL:

ADD UP YOUR TOTAL SCORE FROM QUESTIONS A–L: ________________

SCORE GUIDE:

12–18: You seem to be experiencing very little if any anxiety at the moment.

18–24: You are experiencing some anxiety now.

24–30: Your daily anxiety seems to be getting high.

30–54: You are experiencing very high levels of anxiety at this time.

Keep in mind that the first time you respond to these questions will give you a sense of where you are now. How we experience anxiety and manage our emotions can vary from day to day, week to week, month to month, depending on the stressors in our lives. Be gentle with yourself; this activity is not meant to be judgmental, but exploratory.

Also, you shouldn't compare your anxiety score to anyone else's. Everyone has their own baseline. One person might become highly anxious if they don't meet a deadline; another person might take a missed deadline in stride, trusting that they will finish soon enough. We all come into this world with varying temperaments and a unique personality, along with a physiological baseline related to our sensitivity to stress. The good news is that our stress response is dynamic; we can change it.

SURVEY #2:
HOW DO YOU FEEL WHEN YOU ARE ANXIOUS?

The next step after characterizing your level of anxiety is to ask yourself how anxiety makes you feel. You may recall the wheel of emotions in Chapter Two. There are many names for the negative emotions we associate with anxiety, so being able to identify and label your feelings is a crucial step to bringing conscious awareness to your inner experience and learning to manage anxiety and other negative emotions better. Circle any of the descriptions below that you associate with anxiety.

1) tense
2) strained
3) upset
4) frightened
5) nervous
6) jittery
7) indecisive
8) worried
9) confused
10) restless
11) like a failure
12) inadequate
13) sad
14) disgusted
15) bored
16) dismayed
17) angry
18) terrified
19) distracted
20) pensive
21) annoyed

As you begin to chart your stress response, keep these words and the feelings they evoke in mind. Are some more familiar than others? Are there other words not on the list that you can connect to feelings of anxiety you might be experiencing?

SURVEY #3: WHAT ARE YOUR ANXIETY TRIGGERS?

After acknowledging how anxiety makes you feel, it's helpful to zero in on what in your life tends to trigger anxiety. What tends to send you spiraling into anxiety? What makes your what-if list of worries? What typically causes you to feel worry, dread, or fear?

Some common sources of anxiety, in no certain order, include:

- financial insecurity
- food insecurity or hunger
- friendship or relationship distress, disagreement, or conflict
- social anxiety (Do I fit in? Do I belong? Am I being judged?)
- isolation and loneliness
- disappointment in love or work
- job threat or loss
- children being ill or in trouble
- illness of elderly parent
- death or loss
- personal illness
- lack of sleep
- fear of catching the flu or another virus or contagious infection
- fear of social interaction
- fear of conflict
- fear of medical intervention

What are your top five triggers for worry or anxiety? As you identify your triggers, write them down in a journal or on your smartphone and rank them from most concerning (1) to least concerning (5). And of course, next to the top five triggers write down the most recent situation, thought, or memory that summons the feeling, being as descriptive as possible.

MY TOP 5 ANXIETY TRIGGERS AND HOW THEY MAKE ME FEEL		
THE TRIGGER	HOW IT MAKES ME FEEL	MOST RECENT SITUATION
1.		
2.		
3.		
4.		
5.		
Keep this list on hand, and don't be afraid of it. This knowledge is essential to understanding how to use the rich toolbox of techniques and strategies.		

YOUR SELF-SOOTHERS

When you are anxious or upset what do you typically do to calm yourself? Without overthinking, read through the following common self-soothing techniques. Which ones are familiar to you?

1) Taking a bath at the end of the day
2) Going for drinks with friends
3) Picking up fast food on your way home
4) Eating sweets, such as candy, ice cream, or baked goods
5) Meditating
6) Exercising more or not as much
7) Calling or Zooming with friends
8) Taking frequent naps
9) Going shopping
10) Drinking alcohol alone
11) Smoking weed
12) Gardening
13) Spending time outdoors in nature
14) Baking or cooking
15) Binge-watching TV shows

As a way to determine if these coping strategies are working for you, go to the list of positive/negative coping actions on pages 45–46.

I do not want you to judge yourself. Instead, just ask yourself what, if any, of your go-to ways of coping with stress are helping you. Are any hindering you? Or having unwanted secondary effects? Also, which of these coping strategies are working for you? Which could you do more of?

BUILDING STRESS TOLERANCE

As we've seen, building stress tolerance requires becoming more comfortable with uncomfortable feelings. If we immediately try to mask anxiety, push it away, or deny feeling it, then we miss out on the opportunity to use its arousal and attention for good. A good first step is to simply sit with our feelings and lean into the discomfort or agitation, not away from them. By allowing ourselves to recognize and accept the reality of our discomfort, we do two things: 1) we get accustomed to the feeling and realize that we can indeed "survive" it; and 2) we give ourselves the time and space to make a more conscious decision about how to act or respond. This is exactly how a new, more positive neural pathway is established.

This process involves four steps (one of which you've already done!):

1) Become aware of your emotions. Bring to mind a recent negative feeling, identify it, and let the feeling engulf you.

2) Allow the discomfort. Once you have identified the emotion, allow yourself to be present to how it's making you feel, which, in the case of anxiety, may involve agitation and physical or emotional discomfort.

3) Feel the feelings. Let yourself stay open to the

actual physical or emotional sensation. Allow it, focus on it, don't retreat from it or otherwise try to negate it.

4) Make another choice. Now it's time for your PFC to come online and make a conscious decision to direct this energy toward one of the six uses for anxiety.

Before you can actively shift your anxiety into something productive, you need to create enough space emotionally for the shift to happen. The more you practice these steps, the more automatic they will become and soon they can become your go-to strategy whenever you feel anxiety begin to creep to an uncomfortable level.

HOW ARE YOU DOING MANAGING YOUR EMOTIONS?

We cannot underestimate the power of our emotions. And as we've seen, one of the principal ways we learn to handle stress differently and channel anxiety so that we can benefit from it comes when we can regulate or manage our emotions, especially the negative ones. This next questionnaire simplifies two general strategies for managing difficult emotions: reappraisal, which shows cognitive flexibility and a desire to resolve the discomfort; and suppression, which is seen as a maladaptive way of coping with emotional discomfort. As you go through these questions, be honest with yourself. This is not an exercise in judgment, but rather an opportunity to see how ready and/or willing you are to deal with difficult feelings such as anxiety.

EMOTION REGULATION QUESTIONNAIRE (ERQ)[1]

The Emotion Regulation Questionnaire is designed to assess individual differences in the habitual use of two emotion regulation strategies: cognitive reappraisal and expressive suppression.

For each item, indicate using the numeric scale below whether you strongly disagree (1), are neutral (4), or strongly agree (7).

1 -------- 2 -------- 3 -------- 4 -------- 5 -------- 6 -------- 7

1. ____ ***When I want to feel more positive emotion (such as joy or amusement), I change what I'm thinking about.***

2. ____ ***I keep my emotions to myself.***

3. ____ ***When I want to feel less negative emotion (such as sadness or anger), I change what I'm thinking about.***

4. ____ ***When I am feeling positive emotions, I am careful not to express them.***

5. ____ ***When I'm faced with a stressful situation, I make myself think about it in a way that helps me stay calm.***

6. ____ ***I control my emotions by not expressing them.***

7. ____ ***When I want to feel more positive emotion, I change the way I'm thinking about the situation.***

8. ____ ***I control my emotions by changing the way I think about the situation I'm in.***

9. ____ ***When I am feeling negative emotions, I make sure not to express them.***

10. ____ ***When I want to feel less negative emotion, I change the way I'm thinking about the situation.***

....

To interpret your results, first look at how you responded to questions 1, 3, 5, 7, 8, and 10, which are designed to see how frequently or regularly you reappraise a negative emotion. These questions also reflect your desire to feel positive emotions. For instance, if you responded to questions 1, 3, 5, 7, 8, and 10 with higher scores (between neutral and strongly agree), you tend to manage difficult emotions by thinking about the situation differently. This is an indication of good or adequate emotion regulation. Responding to questions 2, 4, 6, and 9 with lower scores is an indication that in the face of emotions—whether negative or positive—you do not suppress those feelings. This is also a sign of good emotion regulation.

However, responses to the first set of questions with lower indicate a difficulty managing emotions and a need for more cognitive flexibility. Further, high scores for the other set of questions (2, 4, 6, and 9) indicate a tendency to suppress emotions. This, too, is a sign of difficulty with emotion regulation.

....

And that's the goal ahead: to learn how to regulate emotions of all kinds as a way to flip anxiety from bad to good and leverage it for our own positive purposes.

YOUR GOOD ANXIETY TOOLBOX
Tools to Quiet Anxiety

BREATHE

One of the fastest, easiest, and most effective breath-based meditations I have come across is from my friend and breathwork/meditation expert Nicholas Pratley.

Step 1: Find a quiet place to sit.

Step 2: Slowly breathe in deeply for 4 counts.

Step 3: Hold the breath for 6 counts.

Step 4: Slowly breathe out for 8 counts.

Step 5: Repeat 6–8 more times as needed.

There are literally thousands of different kinds of calming breath exercises you can do, including simply breathing normally, as you focus on the details and the feeling of the process. Another example, common in some yoga classes, is alternate nostril breathing. Use the thumb and ring finger of your dominant hand to alternatively block your right or left nostril in the following pattern: First block your right nostril and breathe in on a 4 count through the open left nostril. Next, hold the breath in for a 4 count. Then unblock the right nostril and slowly exhale as you block the left nostril. Start again from the nostril through which you just exhaled. Google and explore at will!

DIVERT YOUR ATTENTION TO SOMETHING POSITIVE

When in the midst of an anxiety-provoking situation, you can train yourself to divert your attention away from that element that is triggering you and focus on something in your life that is positive. Instead of focusing on the big scary public speech you have no way of getting out of, talk to a friend casually about the subject matter. Count ceiling tile squares or try to remember the names of everyone in the room. Stay in the environment you're presently in but find a way to make it feel more familiar. This practice of diverting your attention may sound simple, and it is, but it can also have a strong effect and help you manage anxiety.

CELEBRATE YOUR WINS

One key tool that will help you deal with situations that make you feel anxious is to remind yourself of your wins. How? Spend time appreciating every triumph in your battle to flip bad anxiety to good. Did you survive the interaction? Celebrate it! Did you successfully change or modify the situation to make it less stress-producing? Give yourself a treat—Starbucks for you!

CHOOSE WISELY

Remembering that you have control over what you are exposed to is a great way to sidestep triggers and give you the space to re-appraise. Taking control of your environment—where you work, live, eat, sleep, and spend time and with whom—is a powerful way to offset that feeling that you are not in control of your life or your emotions. Taking control requires you to act consciously and deliberately, not "let things happen to you." Consider this exercise: The next time you find yourself in the presence of someone's bad mood or angry outburst, take a breath and re-mind yourself that his or her bad attitude is not your problem. This may seem overly simple, and yet each time you separate yourself from someone else's mood or situation, you reinforce your own boundaries.

MODIFY THE SITUATION

Some situations will always be triggers for anxiety, so instead of expending energy avoiding or trying to escape (which often leads to maladaptive behaviors), try a new tack: Prepare. The fewer unknowns you're facing, the more control you will have in the situation. For example, if you hate speaking off the cuff, then make sure that any report you have to give in front of a group is fully prepared and written out. Take time to rehearse, visualizing yourself standing or seated with your colleagues, uttering the report aloud. You might send your report to the chair of the meeting for them to read it out, or you might benefit from reading it yourself before the big moment to ensure that you're happy with how it sounds. The idea here is you always have choices in even the most anxiety-provoking situations—especially if you have some time to strategize. This is why it's so important to really get to know your anxiety well so you can better predict and even anticipate the inevitable situations that have the potential to trigger you. The more prepared you are, the more you can control your anxiety.

DISCOVER YOUR ROOTS

Go back to your list of top five anxiety triggers and think about why you have each of those anxieties in the first place. Where do they come from? Who else in your life shares them? Where else in your life do you see those anxieties manifesting? Maybe you inherited your lifelong anxiety over the lack of money from your parents; maybe your social anxiety comes from an embarrassing incident in elementary school. For most of us, even the most general of anxieties paints a specific picture in our minds or brings up a specific example if we think about it long enough, so let that example come to your mind now. Now comes the challenge: Can you reframe that negative event (the bully who made fun of your comment) or that belief (money is hard to come by) and flip it on its head? Can you, for example, accept that negative experience with the bully as a one-off and instead nurture the reframed belief that you have something interesting and important to contribute to conversations? Or can you cultivate the reframed belief that money is plentiful? While it may take more time than the other tools to really implement, even the act of identifying the belief that is at the core of your anxieties is a productive first step.

FUEL YOUR BRAIN

Studies show that when we eat clean, nutritious food and keep ourselves in good blood sugar balance, we are more likely to feel good and think more clearly.[2] Eating is a practice in self-nurturance. On the other hand, denying ourselves food, dieting, and creating a sense of scarcity only diminishes our sense of control and exacerbates our anxiety. Foods that contain healthy fats are shown to calm the brain, and you need that fuel for the rest of this work managing anxiety. So here are two simple strategies that will help you flip your anxiety from bad to good: 1) Make a choice to increase your serving of veggies and decrease your servings of proteins and grains for today; and 2) Add a mood-boosting snack to your diet: avocado toast, salmon avocado toast, granola with blueberries, pecans, pumpkin seeds, walnuts, and toasted oats, or my favorite—organic unsweetened yogurt with cacao nibs sprinkled on top.

HACK YOUR SLEEP

Sleep is essential for optimum mental and physical health, yet recent estimates show that about 30 percent of Americans get only six hours of sleep a night or less. Sleep deprivation leads to a suppressed immune response, an inefficient stress response, higher blood cortisol levels, and an overall difficulty managing emotions. Like so many of us, I have been in a long-term struggle to improve the quality and quantity of my sleep. I tried all the suggestions I could find from the most reputable sources and here is what worked for me.

At first, all I wanted to do was to try a few simple suggestions that I could do easily. I started to eat dinner earlier so I would not be digesting a belly full of food when I went to bed. Next, I made myself drink lots of water early in the day and stopped drinking around six p.m. Third, I made sure I never scrolled on any screen after I went into the bedroom to sleep, and set the temperature in my bedroom to a cool mid-60 degrees. Together these three adjustments accomplished three positive changes to my sleep: my body was more relaxed when I went to bed; I stopped needing to pee in the middle of the night; and I fell asleep more easily in the cooler room.

But two additional actions were big game changers that led to a consistent eight hours of sleep each night:

1) I cut way down on my alcohol consumption. I know this is a difficult one for many, but once you see how much better you feel after you sleep well, cutting down on your favorite drinks doesn't seem nearly as bad!

2) I give myself a full eight hours of time in bed to sleep and don't cut corners because I want to watch another episode of *Bridgerton*. No matter what's on my agenda, I give myself that eight hours of sleep time and my body thanks me for it every day!

Don't get me wrong, I still have bad nights; but I went from six to seven hours a night to a steady eight hours a night with these hacks and I feel better, stronger, and more energized than I have in years!

EXERCISE YOUR WAY TO CALM

Do you know what form of movement gives you the best natural mood boost and anxiety removal? It's different for different people. For me, it's a thirty-minute hard cardio or Tabata workout where I can't quite do everything, but I still try. It's hard, but I feel so proud of myself after and it's a buzz that lasts for the rest of the day.

Now it's your turn. Your challenge is to find the form of physical activity that you are already doing that gives you the biggest mood boost. Is it a power walk? Bike ride? Zumba class? Yoga?

Tango lessons? Just noticing which form of movement (or which inspiring instructor) makes you feel your best is an awareness that you can keep in your back pocket for when you need it. The idea is simply to compare and contrast your own mood explicitly after the range of workouts that you usually do. Which one gives you the biggest mood boost? Keep this in mind so that on a day when you really need a boost, you know which exercise will work best for you.

What if you've been meaning to start moving more and you just haven't gotten around to it? In that case, I would suggest you take a walk and note how it makes you feel. Maybe compare the effect of a ten-minute walk with a twenty-minute walk—something most people can do. Most people will experience a noticeable effect on their mood, specifically boosting energy and feeling more "upbeat" or positive. It is very powerful to get sensitized to the mood boost and anxiety-busting effects of movement so you can use that information strategically in your everyday life.

OLFACTORY RELAXATION

Have you ever noticed that a particular smell can immediately take you back to a specific memory? Olfactory cues are particularly powerful memory stimulants because olfaction is the only sense that has a direct projection to the hippocampus. If there is an olfactory cue that evokes a particularly "warm and fuzzy" memory for you, find it. Is it your mother's perfume or your father's cologne? Is it the smell of a favorite food, or the smell of a particular flower or herb? Find these smells and keep them around to create a kind of olfactory "scene" of warm and fuzzy memories. If the smells that evoke those memories are impossible to get, then try different essential oils to see if they can evoke warm and fuzzy states in you. I always love eucalyptus as an energizer and lavender as a calming agent. If these different scents work for you, use them to evoke the kind of emotion or mood you are seeking. (See also Pracitce Joy Conditioning, page 229.)

Tools That Leverage Your Good Anxiety and Open the Door to Your Superpowers

Build Your Resilience

When you practice resilience regularly, it will be there for you when you need it. Along the way, you will learn to appreciate or even welcome certain kinds of mistakes for all the new information they bring you.

PRACTICE OPTIMISM

If you want to enrich optimism, then this is the hack for you. At the beginning or end of each day (whichever works best for you), think through all those uncertain situations currently in your life—both big and small. *Will that special someone text me back? Will I get a good performance review? Will my kid settle in well in his school?* Now take each of these and visualize the most optimistic, amazing, loving, and lovely outcome to the situation. Not just the "okay" outcome, I mean the best possible outcome you could imagine. This is not to set you up for an even bigger disappointment if he doesn't text back. Instead, it should build the muscle of expecting the positive outcome and might even open up ideas for how to get to that most optimistic outcome—that is, what more you might do to create that outcome of your dreams.

PRACTICE POSITIVE SELF-TWEETING

Lin-Manuel Miranda published a book about the tweets he sends out at the beginning and end of the day.[4] In it, he shares what are essentially upbeat little messages that are funny, singsongy, and generally delightful. I don't know about you, but when I see him interviewed, I see an inherently positive, optimistic person who has a classic activist mindset. How do you get to be that productive and creative? Clearly, part of the answer is positive self-tweeting! The idea here is to boost yourself up at the beginning and end of the day. Tell yourself what you will "crush!" today or what a great job you did at the end of the day. I know this can be difficult for those of us (and I include myself here) who automatically beat ourselves up at the drop of a hat. Instead think about what your number one best supporter in life (spouse, sibling, friend, parent, favorite aunt) would say to you and learn to say or tweet it to yourself!

PUSH YOUR LIMITS

These days it's easier than ever to join a new online class or Instagram Live event featuring a new workout. Just a few months ago, after reading about it in the paper, I joined the Wimbledon champ herself Venus Williams and her mother in an Instagram Live workout where she was using Prosecco bottles as her weights. It was a fantastic and memorable workout. The point is that for free or for only a small fee you can play exercise class roulette and push yourself with whatever you find! The workout may be easy, hard, just your level, or something you've never done before; the point is to push your brain-body to go all in.

IMMERSE YOURSELF IN NATURE

Science has shown again and again that spending time in nature is soothing and restorative. Have you heard of the ancient Japanese art of forest bathing?[5] It's the idea of walking through the forest and just soaking in all the tree-infused oxygen as if you are bathing. Now, I don't have a forest nearby, but I have treated my forays into Central Park as a forest-bathing-like experience and in some of those quiet spots where there aren't that many people around it works just fine. But if forest bathing isn't your thing, find any kind of natural environment in which to spend time. Breathe, relax, and become aware of the sounds, smells, and sights. Use all of your senses to create a heightened awareness of the natural world. This exercise boosts your overall resilience as it acts as a kind of restoration of energy and reset to your equilibrium.

REACH OUT

I remember a particularly bad breakup I went through when I first moved to New York. Two of my best friends, a couple, Susan and Joseph, live in Arizona, and when I called them crying, they immediately invited me to fly out that weekend. I took them up on the invitation. I remember feeling like the luckiest loser on the planet that I had friends who would take care of me. Thinking back, the guy I broke up with was not worth all the drama he caused in my life by far. But I was at a real emotional low point, crying, upset, and not fully in control of my body movements. I was so out of sorts when I arrived, I managed to accidentally slam the door on Joseph's hand when I was getting my bags out of the car. My friend was hosting a small dinner party for some faculty colleagues and I am sure I could have won an award for most depressing party guest ever. I couldn't even fake happy—something I am usually very good at. Looking back on it now, I know that the lesson was not only that I could get through that breakup but also how precious good friends are. They took me in, cleaned me up, and were there for me. That right there was what helped kickstart my recovery from that breakup and I will never forget the love they showed me.

Being able to ask for help, staying connected to friends and family, and actively nurturing supportive, encouraging relationships not only enables you to keep bad anxiety at bay but also shores up the sense that you are not alone—a belief and feeling that is crucial during times of enormous stress, when you need to fall back on your own resilience in order to persevere and maintain your well-being. When we are suffering from loss or other forms of distress, it's natural to withdraw. Indeed, we see this kind of behavior with animals who are in mourning. Yet you also have the power to push yourself into the loving embrace of those who can help take care of you.

....

Treat resilience-building like an experiment. Ask yourself, what is the simplest thing that you do for a friend, that's easy for you to do and that you know would bring them joy? Now do that thing you just thought of and jot down how it makes you feel (that's the experimental part). If you believe all the neuroscience studies, altruism packs a huge dopamine punch, which makes it a powerful way to efficiently build your resilience stores. Make it something that you do easily but that your friend would find novel or interesting. Everyone has something simple and easy they can do for a friend that brings so much more joy than the effort it takes to do it. Baking talent? Car oil change talent? Talent at making a computer or phone work more efficiently? For me, it's doing sheep brain dissections for my friends' kids. I can do it fast, I can make it fun, and I always have lots of fun doing it. I love seeing the reactions of shock, awe, and wonder each and every time. So my dopamine-boosting altruism hack has been to organize a sheep brain dissection party in my lab for the eight- to ten-year-old kids of my friends. Both parents and kids are thrilled (once everyone gets over the ick factor), it takes no more preparation for me than to find the date that everyone is free, and I usually get treated to ice cream after! Even if you don't have sheep brain dissection up your sleeve, spend some time thinking about what your special gift can be and give it!

Enhance Your Performance and Get into Flow

PRACTICE MAKES PERFECT

Explore the power of practice makes perfect. Dedicate the next week to the practice of some skill you have been wanting to work on but have not found the time. Try to practice for at least twenty minutes each day, wherever and whenever you can fit it in. Make sure to keep track of your practice sessions so that you can note your learning curve and performance curve after this week of practice. Lather, rinse, repeat!

FAKE IT TILL YOU MAKE IT FLOW

This exercise is a wonderful way to bring the spirit of flow into your life before it emerges organically. In other words, fake it till you make it! For this one to work, it's important you do this exercise privately, with no one else watching to give any "helpful" comments. Here is how it works. Pick an activity or skill you are not good at right now but have a secret desire to be better at. For me, it's singing. Next, find a private space and just start singing your favorite song as soulfully as you can with no care about the quality of the product. Instead focus on the joy of the effort. I think much of our flow is squelched before it starts by the perfectionist in us comparing what comes out of our mouths to Whitney Houston or Beyoncé or what gets drawn on the page to Matisse or Basquiat. This is actually an exercise to see if you can create a sense of flow from mindful and joyful engagement. I guarantee that if you try this exercise regularly, not only will your fake flow turn into real flow but the quality of your sessions will also noticeably improve. Other activities that you can apply this to include sports (hitting tennis balls against a wall or against a machine or hitting golf balls at a driving range), drawing, as mentioned above, cooking, sewing, knife sharpening, housecleaning, or dog training. What if you could generate flow just by fully and mindfully enjoying the activities of your life? This exercise, together with the cultivation of micro flow, should up the flow in your life considerably as it did in mine.

CREATE NEW MICRO FLOW MOMENTS

The idea here is to explore and create new and different ways to experience micro flow—that is, those brief moments where you feel in sync with yourself and clearheaded about how you're experiencing the moment. How do you do this? Start with keeping a feel-good journal for a week or two. Every time you experience something—anything—that makes you feel good, or loved, or appreciated, or empowered, just write it down. Now look at what is on that list. Are there themes? Are there times or areas of your life that led to those feel-good entries? While some of these may have already been on your micro flow list, some may not. Now look at the themes or areas in your life that provide those feel-good moments. Maybe they are associated with socializing or with alone time. Use these themes to help create even more experiences of micro flow in your life. You can also look for holes in your feel-good list. Maybe none include book reading, movie watching, or other activities you know you enjoy. These may be areas to explore to enhance micro flow.

PRACTICE JOY CONDITIONING

We all know that one scary experience on a particularly dark street (an attempted mugging, for example) will keep you away from that location for a long time. This is an example of fear conditioning, dependent on the amygdala, where the location where the bad thing happened (that dark street) is now automatically associated with an intense fear response that can be very difficult to get rid of. Well, it turns out that the amygdala can also facilitate conditioning to positive moods and emotions, what I will call "joy conditioning." While fear conditioning has evolved to be powerful and automatic to help keep us safe, joy conditioning can be used to expand our sense of well-being on a daily basis (particularly on those days when anxiety is high). Here is how it works. Choose an experience from your past that has two key components: First, it made you feel wonderful and makes you want to revisit that feeling, and second, there is a reproducible olfactory sensation associated with the memory. (Here you are taking advantage of the fact that our memories for particular odors last because of the strong connection between our olfactory system and our long-term memory system centered on the hippocampus.)

My example comes from a particularly memorable yoga class I attended. I felt great during that class, flowing through my up dogs, down dogs, and even flipping my dog like a pro. At the end of that sweat-infused class, I settled down for everyone's favorite part of yoga class—savasana. As I was lying there snuggled deep into my yoga mat, unexpectedly the instructor came by, waved her lavender cream–slathered hands in front of my nose, and proceeded to give me one of the most luscious five-second neck massages I have ever experienced. I was in heaven. I also note that I naturally think back to that moment when I smell lavender hand cream, suggesting that my brain automatically created that association between lavender hand cream and the neck massage–enhanced savasana (i.e., joy conditioning). So, I just take that last step of walking around with a small bottle of lavender essential oil and when I want or need a dose of joy or flow in my day, I simply crack open my little bottle and re-create that moment. You can do this with an essential oil or other scent that takes you back to a wonderful memory. Again, this works best with an olfactory-based cue because the olfactory system has a particularly intimate relationship with the hippocampus (the structure essential for creating new long-term memories), and as a consequence it is particularly easy to connect or associate a scent with a particular moment or event in your life. Explore and use the memories you find to help bring more joy to your day. Using your own joyful life experiences to enhance your life may become your new favorite thing!

ACCELERATE AN ACTIVIST MINDSET

THE MINDSET CHECK-IN

Without thinking about it too much, quickly write up to ten short phrases describing how you feel about yourself right now (e.g., frustrated, judgmental, kind, annoyed, loving, angry, grateful, etc.) and why.

1. ______________________________

____

2. ______________________________

____

3. ______________________________

____

4. ______________________________

____

5. ______________________________

____

6. ______________________________

____

7. ______________________________

____

8. ______________________________

____

9. ______________________________

____

10. ______________________________

____

Now, with no judgment at all (this is critical!), look at your list and circle all the positive words on it. Next, expand on these positive things you feel about yourself. Why do you feel this way? How do these features about yourself make you feel? Go as deep as you can to really understand and appreciate the most positive aspects of your self-assessment. If the positive words on your list were not as abundant as you might want them to be, never fear! Move on to hack number two to quickly remedy that.

TRANSFORM YOUR NEGATIVE SELF-TALK

Next, focus on your top two negative feelings about yourself from the list above, as we are going to transform them by using an activist mindset. I'll list just two common ways people are hard on or frustrated with themselves and give some examples of how these might be transformed.

1. Annoyed because of my lack of progress on my career goals. This common annoyance or frustration can be transformed by focusing on what you know you do best in your career—it could be networking, report writing, people or money management. The idea here is to dig deeper to find the productive and positive aspect of this area in your life. Now focus here. If your old mindset was "I am constantly annoyed because I just can't get ahead in my job as fast as I would like," change it to "I know that by focusing on my major strengths of X and Y [from your list above] and learning to strengthen some of my weaknesses, I can get ahead at work."
2. Frustrated at my inability to find a partner. Bring to mind your most valued aspects of a life-partner

relationship. You might have experienced them as part of a previous romantic relationship, with a close friendship (e.g., the trust I've always had with my dear friend Paula), or seen and admired them in others, including your parents or other couples you have known well. Instead of focusing on what you don't have, change your mindset to building a picture of the major elements that you want. What do you want a partner to bring to your life? What dynamic are you looking for in a partnership? Thinking about the building blocks you want to use for a future relationship helps set up a strong framework for knowing how to evaluate future partners. This visualization also enables you to shift away from the lack of something valued in your life and moves it toward building out the elements you are looking for so you will be able to better spot someone great when they come along.

SELF-APPRECIATION 101

This tool is simple, but I recommend that you use it regularly and often. It is taking a moment to appreciate all the blessings in your life. Try to focus here on the ones you may be taking for granted (someone on your team that always has the solution for you, or your home and how it shelters you every day). Try to have one appreciative thought an hour, even if it's as small as how much you like the pen you're using. This exercise is one that will also help get your juices flowing for developing your own set of activist mindset shifts that will help you tackle your most pressing, inspiring, and inspired life goals.

STRETCH AND STRENGTHEN YOUR MINDSET

The more you work your muscles, the stronger they get, and the more fluid and refined your movements become. In many senses the brain works the same way—the neural networks and pathways that we use all the time get stronger, more efficient, and more nimble the more we use them. As we've seen, mindset is more than a temperament or personality trait toward openness, flexibility, and optimism. We all have the power to retrain our view of ourselves to become more growth-oriented. How do we build the neural "muscle" of an activist mindset? The answer is simply by using it as much as possible.

One of the best ways to "flex" your cognitive flexibility "muscle" is to practice learning from your mistakes, just as you did when learning how to develop an activist mindset. A lot of people have a running tally of the big and small mistakes they've made on a particular day—for some, that list can be the focal point of a lot of bad anxiety and proof that they're just not good at something. But instead of worrying over the list, we can actually use it to our advantage. At the end of the day, consciously think through all new insights or learning that came from the moment that felt like a misstep or faux pas. Certainly, all mistakes are not created equal and not all will provide life-altering insights. Sometimes, this extra consideration might make you realize that the incident wasn't a mistake at all. Other times, you will be surprised at what little gifts of knowledge and even wisdom come from consistently assessing the lessons learned from your mistakes. Some of my favorite examples are when some deficit or lack creates something new and unexpected. This could be as simple as paying attention to why you keep hitting a tennis ball into the net when returning a serve. At first, you keep repeating the same mistake; no matter how much you want to hit it over the net, the ball doesn't make it over. Then a teacher points out that the way the racket face meets the ball sends it downward not upward. You adjust and now the balls are flying through the air, over the net, but too high and out of bounds. You adjust again. After weeks of tennis lessons, you finally understand how you need to hold the racket and stroke the ball to control your swing and the direction of the ball. Managing anxiety is incredibly similar. Once you identify for yourself what your objectives are, you will keep adjusting your reactions until you're headed in the direction you want to go.

A more subtle, complicated example of how to learn from a mistake might entail revisiting a time when you made a doozie of a faux pas—one that made you cringe or you've actively tried to forget. This is where visualization can again be a powerful tool. Perhaps it was when you forgot your boss's name at a work event. Instead of remembering the event in shame and embarrassment, revisit it and reimagine the scenario going smoothly—you remember his name, make an amusing remark, and everything goes well. By re-creating the scene in your mind, you are actually creating a new memory that has the power to override your feelings about what happened. You're not changing history, but you are able to clear the path that is currently blocked by the memory of the embarrassing moment. Added bonus: You'll never forget her name again!

Amplify Your Attention and Productivity

RECAST YOUR WHAT-IF LIST

Your what-if list is that annoying list of worries that interrupts your thoughts, causes you to procrastinate, and otherwise interferes with your well-being. *What if I don't ace that next [fill in the blank: report, essay, grant, sales pitch, etc.]? What if I lose my job? What if I don't lose that extra ten pounds?* Most of us have a cache of worries that gnaw at us, and often they are stubborn and not necessarily realistic. So how do we stop these worries from taking over? Recent studies have shown two strategies yield powerful, reliable outcomes. In particular, when people either visualize a positive outcome of a worry and/or verbally name an alternative outcome to the what-if playlist, not only does the experience of worry (i.e., anxiety) lessen but people also experience "an increased perceived ability to cope."[6] In other words, they distance themselves enough from the worry to realize they can handle it.

So try this exercise. It's simple, but its power comes from its repetition. I suggest you put aside at least a week to do this self-experiment, repeating the exercise once a day. It's also important to write down your experience.

1. Bring to mind one of your common what-if worries.

2. For five minutes, focus solely on your breathing. If your mind wanders, just come back to your breath. You may want to use a timer to make sure you persist for the allotted five minutes.

3. After this exercise, return to the selected item on your what-if list and do one of two things:

    i. Close your eyes and visualize a positive outcome to the worry (e.g. all your friends and colleagues coming up to you after your talk to tell you how good it was and how it was the best talk they have ever heard you give).

ii. Close your eyes and say aloud what that positive outcome is (e.g. say to yourself, "After my talk, my colleagues as well as my advisor all come up to me to congratulate me on a superb talk").

When you go to record your notes from a "session," think about how you felt after the breathing step and then again after the visualization or verbal step. You may also want to experiment with different items on your list. I cannot promise that the worries on your list will disappear, but I do predict that you will begin to build up a tolerance to them. You may feel more separate from them and begin to gain a bit more objectivity about them.

FOCUS ON FOCUS

There is always something we need to get done. This exercise can help you become aware of how your own focused attention works and also build it up at the same time.

Here is how it works:

- The next time you are at work or home working on a project that needs to get done soon, give your-self ten minutes to focus on the task. During that time, no other activities are allowed including answering or looking at your phone, surfing the Web, checking your favorite news station, or playing with your pet.
- If you made it through the whole ten minutes, give yourself a pat on the back, a short break if needed, and start again.
- If you suddenly find yourself watching YouTube, for instance, in the middle of your ten-minute focus

challenge, simply note down what the distraction was and start your ten-minute clock again. Don't punish yourself.

This exercise will help you become aware of what distracts you and possibly why. Also note what the limits of your personal focus challenge are—can you go fifteen or thirty minutes? And what happens when you get tired? The latter will indicate when you should be giving yourself a break or calling it a day for the high-attention activities.

CHANGE YOUR ENVIRONMENT

One of the best ways to give yourself a boost of attention when bad anxiety is starting to mount is to simply change your environment. And if you add in some exercise, you amplify the effect. Walking at a good clip can do wonders not only for your mood but for your attention as well. Enhance this strategy by adding a purpose to your walk: Choose a beautiful or enjoyable destination, invite a friend along for support, or make it an extra-long walk that you would typically do either in your supermarket, mall, or even the airport!

STICKY MEDITATION

If you read my first book, *Healthy Brain, Happy Life*,[7] you know how hard it was for me to start a regular meditation practice. I tried everything from guided meditations to classes to YouTube lessons. Nothing worked until I was shown a tea meditation. In tea meditation, you combine an open-monitoring meditation, where you become aware of your thoughts and feelings, with the brewing and drinking of tea. For me, the ritual of brewing delicious tea in a real teapot somehow gave the experience of meditation a rhythm and purpose it never had before.

Here's how it works:

- Set up a place at a table or other comfortable spot and arrange a teapot of boiling water, another teapot (personal size) containing a sufficient amount of loose tea for at least three cups, and your choice of teacup.
- Pour some of the boiling water into the teapot.
- Sit quietly as the tea steeps.
- Carefully pour yourself some tea.
- Drink the tea, savoring its flavor and the sensation of the tea warming your throat and belly. As you drink the tea or wait for the next cup to steep, you can also focus on your surroundings. I always do my tea meditation near many of my houseplants and spend quiet time just observing them. If you are sitting outside, observe nature.
- Repeat this ritual until all the water has been steeped in the teapot.

This daily morning tea meditation was the end of my search for a way into meditation. I loved and, in fact, *needed* the ritual in my life. While I don't actually seek out other forms of meditation, I sometimes try to include loving-kindness and compassion approaches during my tea meditation. For example, I focus on people or animals that bring up the strongest feelings of love, kindness, and compassion, and then (if I feel like it) try to extend those same feelings to other people in my life for whom my feelings of loving-kindness and compassion are less strong. Most mornings I just try to focus on how I am feeling in my body and mind, just letting the fleeting thoughts that try to attract my attention—"What time is my first appointment? Did I hit send on that email last night?"—float past me.

FOCUS YOUR ATTENTION WITH BODY WRITING

Another great way to stay present and train your brain to focus on the now is a regular writing practice. Waking up in the morning or right before going to bed are perfect times to empty your mind onto the page. This exercise will also support your meditation practice.

Here's how it works:

- Take five minutes to write in your journal or on any scrap of paper lying around. (I recommend writing this out rather than typing because it makes you go more slowly and therefore makes the process more contemplative and mindful.)
- Write out exactly how you feel in your body right now. You can start with your feet and work your way up with simple descriptions (strong, powerful, sore, tight—whatever you feel) or focus on one part of your body or your breath.

Try and stay focused on how you are feeling physically to better ground you in the moment. It doesn't matter if you finish this in five minutes or even if you can read everything you wrote (sometimes I can't!). The point is to use this exercise to help you focus on the here and now.

Create Creativity

DELVE INTO YOUR ANXIETY

Have you ever come up with a solution or a work-around because you were under pressure and that was just the first or only thing that came to mind but it worked great? Well, that means you've probably already used at least an aspect of your bad anxiety for creativity. Even if the solution was not the most elegant, some anxiety-fueled fixes are just the thing to get you over the hump! Think about all the times that you came up with a quick-fix solution and write down your favorite examples. For instance, I remember a time when I was having major strain in my upper back and neck because of the way I was hunching over my computer tapping away all day. It was especially bad at home where I do a lot of my book writing. I really wanted a standing desk for my home, but I just didn't have enough room in my apartment. I had researched the perfect one, but not only was it way too expensive, it was also too big for my small space. Yet all the while my shoulders were getting more and more hunched over. My solution: paper towels. It turns out that two full rolls of paper towels on my dining room table not only bring my computer up to the perfect height for standing but can easily be put away in the kitchen when I'm not standing and typing. Now it's your turn: What's a source of daily irritation or anxiety in your life that makes you feel like you're hitting a wall? How can you separate your feelings about the problem from your desire to find a solution? Allowing yourself to first focus on how the anxiety is making you feel may help you come up with alternative solutions. Giving yourself permission to experience anxiety, annoyance, or even anger can often lead to an opening to create or invent something really useful in your life. This exercise just may help you appreciate ways you have already used experiences of bad anxiety to solve a problem creatively!

WRITE A NEW STORY

I hope that one takeaway from this book is the realization that every challenging, even tragic, anxiety-filled situation can be a launchpad for creativity. In this exercise, take a challenging situation from your past—a bad breakup is often a good example. Choose one that is far enough in your past so that you have some perspective on it and it is not causing any acute pain or anxiety. Now write a story about that breakup that includes the good parts—perhaps how the relationship began. Then, as you move toward describing the end or when the tables turned, describe the events as if you were an observer. Finally, identify the best aspects of that relationship, including all the life lessons you learned about yourself and about how relationships work and how they are serving you today. This is a version of a reframing experiment, but the story allows you to create something new to commemorate a difficult learning experience in your life.

PRACTICE MAKING A SILK PURSE FROM A SOW'S EAR: DELIBERATE CREATIVITY

This is your moment to practice deliberate creativity by working your attention network. Take either a real problem from your personal life or your work life that you are trying to solve or some skill that you are trying to improve. Now use your focused attention network based in your prefrontal cortex to systematically explore and research the problem or skill. Interview others about how they might have seen it solved before; look up all the related solutions you can find. Spend time on solving this problem so you think through each step in a deeper way than you've done before. You might even want to model different solutions. The idea is to use this kind of deliberate, attention-centric approach to explore this category of creativity. Come up with at least three different solutions to review.

MAKING A SILK PURSE FROM A SOW'S EAR: PART II

Now take a different problem that you wish to solve (e.g., how to optimize meal planning to avoid wasting food, or how to make your home footprint greener). This time use a spontaneous creativity approach, letting your mind wander (using your DMN network, aka your mind-wandering network) to approach the problem more indirectly. Note that the last exercise and this one both require key aspects of good anxiety. Namely, a drive or energy to solve problems creatively and control over your attention network to either deploy it in a more direct way for the deliberate form of creative problem solving or in a more indirect way to focus on other ideas that might inspire a solution for the current problem.

LUCID DREAMING

For centuries dreams have been considered sources of inspiration and creativity. One particular form of dreams, known as lucid dreams, can be consciously practiced and used to trigger more creative thoughts or insights. Formally, a lucid dream is one in which the dreamer is aware that he or she is dreaming. Although Stephen LaBerge, a psychophysiologist, has done considerable research investigating lucid dreaming and wrote a book that offers detailed ways to practice and enhance this type of wakeful dreaming,[8] you can use a simplified version as a hack for your own lucid dreaming experience.

- Decide before going to sleep what you wish to dream about; have a goal or intention.
- Meditate on this intention and begin to go consciously to sleep.
- As you move toward sleep, visualize yourself in the scene of the intention or goal.

- Bring to mind specific details and keep focused on them; this will help build your memory of them.
- When you wake—in the night or morning—write down your dream in as much detail as you can.

The more you practice these steps, the more your brain will begin to pay attention to your dreams.

IT'S TIME FOR A MASSAGE!

A 2012 study[9] showed that a massage increases oxytocin in humans, and since oxytocin can help lower stress, what better way to increase oxytocin and decrease stress for your brain? While that study did not determine if it was any kind of stimulation that would work (would an airport chair massage work just as well?) or if it was specifically the human contact, if you are looking for a good excuse to get that next massage, this is it! The power of touch is irrefutable. It's why newborns are put skin-to-skin on a mother's chest; it's why holding hands warms the heart; it's why getting one's feet rubbed feels so relaxing. Physical touch releases both oxytocin and dopamine—some of the most powerful feel-good brain-body chemicals!

HUG IT OUT

If massage increases oxytocin levels, it should not be surprising that other kinds of physical touch, including hugging, cuddling, kissing, all the way up to sex (just like the prairie voles!), increase oxytocin in the brain and make you feel good. Sometimes you really do just need a hug, so don't be afraid to ask for one!

LAUGH OUT LOUD

Laughing increases oxytocin release as well, so if a social laugh is not appealing, use a funny movie, stand-up comedy show, TV show, or even your favorite home movies to give yourself a laugh. Give yourself a laughing weekend, only choosing activities designed to make you laugh! You can give yourself a micro bout of laughter in all sorts of ways: Check out parent TikToks; watch old *SNL* clips on YouTube; find bloopers of movie scenes; discover new stand-up comics testing their mettle on Comedy Central or other stations.

Use Your Anxiety to Boost Your Social Muscle

Social intelligence can be developed. Here are a few simple but powerful ways to tap into your empathy, connect to others, and hone your compassion, all while using your anxiety.

- Triggered by a bad memory of any kind? First, remind yourself about someone you are truly grateful for in your life (this person can be totally unrelated to that anxiety-provoking memory) and take the time to send a handwritten thank-you note—with a stamp and everything—describing why you are grateful to this person. It can be very short and sweet, but I guarantee it will not only be appreciated by your recipient but also strengthen your connection with that person.
- Worried about money? Donate to a good cause that really needs the money to put your money worries in perspective.
- Experiencing FOMO? Send three friendly texts just to say hello or ask a question.
- Have testing anxiety? Invite someone to join you for a study session over Zoom.

- Have job worries? Ask someone more senior to be your mentor and advisor for your plans for advancement.

Do you sense a theme here? To quote Diana Ross, "Reach out and touch somebody's hand. Make this world a better place if you can." Communication is the key, and if face-to-face (or Zoom-to-Zoom) is too scary then go old-school with a letter or new-school with a text. Do you know how good an unexpected text from a friend saying that they miss you feels? Give that to someone else and pay attention to how it feels if you get a response!

THE SCIENCE OF SMILING

A fast and easy way to flex your social muscle is to smile. And there is science behind this hack as well. A study from the University of Kansas[10] showed that relative to people who did not smile, people who were asked to "fake" smile during a series of stressful tasks had a lower stress response; the bigger the fake smile, the lower the stress response. In fact, the researchers showed that even pushing up lips into a smile with sticks creates a lower stress response than not smiling at all. While the specific mechanism of this response was not examined, it has been replicated and may be similar to the immediate effect of deep breathing on your stress and anxiety levels. Deep breathing mimics and activates the parasympathetic system that serves to decrease stress and anxiety levels. Similarly, even fake smiling may be able to activate those same "rest and digest" responses in your nervous system. The bottom line: Grinning and bearing it may actually help you sail through your bouts of anxiety better than you realize.

A FINAL NOTE OF LOVE

Anxiety is Your Superpower has always been a book about how embracing all aspects of anxiety, including all the information it teaches us about ourselves, offers us a path to a more fulfilling, creative, less stressful life. It is my hope that you can now see that anxiety can be a power, not a curse. I also hope you can see that, from a scientific perspective, you have much more control over your thoughts, feelings, and behaviors than you may think. Indeed, the research, stories, and exercises in this book all attest to how flexible and plastic our brains truly are and how this plasticity, this drive to learn and adapt, is captured and fueled by good anxiety. The positive mindset, the increased productivity, the compassion, the flow of performance, the ignited creativity, and the supercharged resilience—these are all the extras that come with the awareness and owning of all that our brains and anxiety can do for us and others. But there's one final superpower that I want to share with you: love.

The deaths of my father and brother have forever changed me and my life. One of the most immediate effects has been the strengthening of the bond with my mom, sister-in-law, and niece. There is no other way to say it: We are closer now. There is a new shared bond, a deeper, more "exposed" kind of love and a deeper, very conscious appreciation that has taken root. This love has cascaded over to all my family and friends. It has also changed my priorities in big and small ways—from how I decide to spend my time (more time on laughter with friends and family; less time locked in my lab alone, reviewing research) to what I want to create in this world (something that helps people use their brains to maximize their talents).

This enriched capacity for love also made this book suddenly much clearer in my mind and therefore easier to write. I have realized how much of my love for my brother was actually under the surface and not apparent to me before he passed. Perhaps it was hidden by the remnants of sibling rivalry or some other kind of lingering childishness on my part. His death has shown me just how profoundly meaningful that love really was.

The old adage that you never quite realize how special people really are until they are gone is, for me, undeniably true. On the other hand, I think I may never have been able to experience the depth of my love for my brother if I had not actually lost him. The cause of all the pain and anguish I felt was both an expression of my love and also the essence of what allowed me to find this new, expansive superpower of love in my life. That love has also been the inspiration for each and every one of the anxiety-based superpowers in this book.

I've come to know that there is a depth, a knowing, and a wisdom that comes from the losses and hurts and trials and tribulations of our lives. And its highest embodiment is a deeper sense of love for and about one's own life. In the end, I realize that I continue to grow and evolve as a person not despite the loss of my father and brother but, in fact, because of it.

I hope you are inspired to feel the love, embrace the love, and spread the love. In my opinion, love is our most powerful personal superpower; it is beyond measure, to be used abundantly and exuberantly each and every day for the rest of our lives.

Dr. Wendy Suzuki
April 4, 2021

ACKNOWLEDGMENTS

I am so grateful to my coauthor and writing partner, Billie Fitzpatrick, for her wisdom, patience, and inspired writing abilities. Thank you to my extraordinary book agent, Yfat Reiss Gendell, for her creativity and ever-present badass-ness. And thank you to our wonderful editor, Leah Miller, for her positive energy, vision, and superb editing abilities.

NOTES

PART ONE

Chapter One

1 Joseph LeDoux, *Anxious: Using the Brain to Understand and Treat Fear and Anxiety* (New York: Penguin Press, 2015).

2 Robert M. Sapolsky, "Why Stress Is Bad for Your Brain," *Science* 273 (5276), 1996: 749–50, doi:10.1126/science.273.5276.749; Robert M. Sapolsky, *Why Zebras Don't Get Ulcers* (New York: W. H. Freeman, 1998).

3 Jack P. Shonkoff and Deborah A. Phillips, eds., *From Neurons to Neighborhoods: The Science of Early Childhood Development* (Washington, DC: National Academies Press, 2000).

4 Website of the Anxiety & Depression Association of America, https://adaa.org.

Chapter Two

1 Mark R. Rosenzweig, David Krech, Edward L. Bennett, and Marian C. Diamond, "Effects of Environmental Complexity and Training on Brain Chemistry and Anatomy: A Replication and Extension," *Journal of Comparative and Physiological Psychology* 55 (4), 1962: 429–37, doi:10.1037/h0041137.

2 Tiffany A. Ito, Jeff T. Larsen, N. Kyle Smith, and John T. Cacioppo, "Negative Information Weighs More Heavily on the Brain: The Negativity Bias in Evaluative Categorizations," *Journal of Personality and Social Psychology* 75 (4), 1998: 887–900, doi:10.1037//0022-3514.75.4.887.

3 Robert Plutchik, "A General Psychoevolutionary Theory of Emotion," in *Emotion: Theory, Research, and Experience, Volume 1: Theories of Emotion*, Robert Plutchik and Henry Kellerman, eds., (New York: Academic Press, 1980), 3–33.

4 Jeremy P. Jamieson, Alia J. Crum, J. Parker Goyer, Marisa E. Marotta, and Modupe Akinola, "Optimizing Stress Responses with Reappraisal and Mindset Interventions: An Integrated Model," *Anxiety Stress and Coping* 31 (3) 2018: 245–61, doi:10.1080/10615806.2018.144261.

5 James J. Gross, "Emotion Regulation: Past, Present, Future," *Cognition and Emotion*, Volume 13: 1999;13:551–573.

6 James J. Gross, "Antecedent- and Response-Focused Emotion Regulation: Divergent Consequences for Experience, Expression, and Physiology," *Journal of Personality and Social Psychology* 74 (1), 1998: 224–37, doi:10.1037//0022-3514.74.1.224; James J. Gross, ed., *Handbook of Emotion Regulation*, 2nd ed. (New York: Guilford Press, 2014).

7 Josh M. Cisler, Bunmi O. Olatunji, Matthew T. Feldner, and John P. Forsyth, "Emotion Regulation and the Anxiety Disorders: An Integrative Review," *Journal of Psychopathology and Behavioral Assessment* 32 (1), 2010: 68–82, doi:10.1007/s10862-009-9161-1.

Chapter Three

1 Elizabeth I. Martin, Kerry J. Ressler, Elisabeth Binder, and Charles B. Nemeroff, "The Neurobiology of Anxiety Disorders: Brain Imaging, Genetics, and Psychoneuroendocrinology," *Psychiatric Clinics of North America* 32 (3), 2009: 549–75, doi:10.1016/j.psc.2009.05.004; Rainer H. Straub and Maurizio Cutolo, "Psychoneuroimmunology—Developments in Stress Research," *Wiener Medizinische Wochenschrift* 168 (3–4), 2018: 76–84, doi:10.1007/s10354-017-0574-2.

PART TWO

Chapter Four

1 Karen J. Parker and Dario Maestripieri, "Identifying Key Features of Early Stressful Experiences that Produce Stress Vulnerability and Resilience in Primates," *Neuroscience & Biobehavioral Reviews* 35 (7), 2011: 1466–83, doi:10.1016/j.neubiorev.2010.09.003.

2 American Psychological Association, "Building Your Resilience," https://www.apa.org/topics/resilience.

3 Theodore M. Brown and Elizabeth Fee, "Walter Bradford Cannon: Pioneer Physiologist of Human Emotions," *American Journal of Public Health* 92 (10), 2002: 1594–95.

4 Hideo Uno, Ross Tarara, James G. Else, Mbaruk A. Suleman, and Robert M. Sapolsky, "Hippocampal Damage Associated with Prolonged and Fatal Stress in Primates," *Journal of Neuroscience* 9 (5), 1989: 1705–11, doi:10.1523/JNEUROSCI.09-05-01705.1989.

5 Gang Wu, Adriana Feder, Hagit Cohen, Joanna J. Kim, Solara Calderon, et al., "Understanding Resilience," *Frontiers in Behavioral Neuroscience* 7 (10), 2013, doi:10.3389/fnbeh.2013.00010.

6 Richard Famularo, Robert Kinscherff, and Terence Fenton, "Psychiatric Diagnoses of Maltreated Children: Preliminary Findings," *Journal of the American Academy of Child & Adolescent Psychiatry* 31 (5), 1992: 863–67, doi:10.1097/00004583-199209000-00013.

7 Louise S. Ethier, Jean-Pascal Lemelin, and Carl Lacharité, "A Longitudinal Study of the Effects of Chronic Maltreatment on Children's Behavioral and Emotional Problems," *Child Abuse & Neglect* 28 (12), 2004: 1265–78, doi:10.1016/j.chiabu.2004.07.006.

8 Jungeen Kim and Dante Cicchetti, "Longitudinal Trajectories of Self-System Processes and Depressive Symptoms Among Maltreated and Nonmaltreated Children," *Child Development* 77 (3), 2006: 624–39, doi:10.1111/j.1467-8624.2006.00894.x.

9 Celia C. Lo and Tyrone C. Cheng, "The Impact of Childhood Maltreatment on Young Adults' Substance Abuse," *The Amer-*

ican Journal of Drug and Alcohol Abuse 33 (1), 2007: 139–46, doi:10.1080/00952990601091119.

10 Cathy Spatz Widom and Michael G. Maxfield, "A Prospective Examination of Risk for Violence Among Abused and Neglected Children," *Annals of the New York Academy of Sciences* 794, 1996: 224–37, doi:10.1111/j.1749-6632.1996.tb32523.x.

11 Eamon McCrory, Stephane A. De Brito, and Essi Viding, "Research Review: The Neurobiology and Genetics of Maltreatment and Adversity," *The Journal of Child Psychology and Psychiatry* 51 (10), 2010: 1079–95, doi:10.1111/j.1469-7610.2010.02271.x.

12 Michael D. De Bellis, Matcheri S. Keshavan, Duncan B. Clark, B. J. Casey, Jay N. Giedd, et al., "Developmental Traumatology, Part II: Brain Development," *Biological Psychiatry* 45 (10), 1999: 1271–84, doi:10.1016/s0006-3223(99)00045-1.

13 Martin H. Teicher, Jacqueline A. Samson, Carl M. Anderson, and Kyoko Ohashi, "The Effects of Childhood Maltreatment on Brain Structure, Function and Connectivity," *Nature Reviews Neuroscience* 17 (10), 2016: 652–66, doi:10.1038/nrn.2016.111; Fu Lye Woon, Shabnam Sood, and Dawson W. Hedges, "Hippocampal Volume Deficits Associated with Exposure to Psychological Trauma and Posttraumatic Stress Disorder in Adults: A Meta-Analysis," *Progress in Neuro-Psychopharmacology and Biological Psychiatry* 34 (7), 2010: 1181–88, doi:10.1016/j.pnpbp.2010.06.016.

14 Jack P. Shonkoff and Deborah A. Phillips, eds., *From Neurons to Neighborhoods: The Science of Early Childhood Development* (Washington, DC: National Academies Press, 2000).

15 Jack P. Shonkoff, W. Thomas Boyce, and Bruce S. McEwen, "Neuroscience, Molecular Biology, and the Childhood Roots of Health Disparities: Building a New Framework for Health Promotion and Disease Prevention," *JAMA* 301 (21), 2009: 2252–59, doi:10.1001/jama.2009.754.

16 Dominic J. C. Wilkinson, Jane M. Thompson, and Gavin W. Lambert, "Sympathetic Activity in Patients with Panic Disorder at

Rest, Under Laboratory Mental Stress, and During Panic Attacks," *JAMA Psychiatry* 55 (6), 1998: 511–20, doi:10.1001/archpsyc.55.6.511.

17 Flurin Cathomas, James W. Murrough, Eric J. Nestler, Ming-Hu Han, and Scott J. Russo, "Neurobiology of Resilience: Interface Between Mind and Body," *Biological Psychiatry* 86 (6), 2019: 410–20, doi:10.1016/j.biopsych.2019.04.011.

18 M. E. Seligman, "Depression and Learned Helplessness," in *The Psychology of Depression: Contemporary Theory and Research*, eds. R. J. Friedman and M. M. Katz (London: John Wiley & Sons, 1974), 83–125.

19 J. Brockhurst, C. Cheleuitte-Nieves, C. L. Buckmaster, A. F. , and D. M. Lyons, "Stress Inoculation Modeled in Mice," *Translational Psychiatry* 5 (3), 2015: e537, doi: 10.1038/tp.2015.34; PMID: 25826112; PMCID: PMC4354359.

20 Gang Wu, Adriana Feder, Hagit Cohen, Joanna J. Kim, Solara Calderon, et al., "Understanding Resilience," *Frontiers in Behavioral Neuroscience* 7, 2013: 10, doi:10.3389/fnbeh.2013.00010.

Chapter Five

1 Malcolm Gladwell, *Outliers: The Story of Success* (New York: Little, Brown, 2008).

2 Mihaly Csikszentmihalyi, *Flow: The Psychology of Optimal Experience* (New York: HarperCollins, 1991).

3 Ibid.

4 Jeanne Nakamura and Mihaly Csikszentmihalyi, "Flow Theory and Research," in *The Oxford Handbook of Positive Psychology*, eds. Shane J. Lopez and C. R. Snyder (New York: Oxford University Press, 2009), 89–105.

5 Robert Yerkes and John D. Dodson, "The Relation of Strength of Stimulus to Rapidity of Habit Formation," *Journal of Comparative Neurology & Psychology* 18 (1908): 459–82, doi:10.1002/cne.920180503.

6 Sian Beilock, *Choke: What the Secrets of the Brain Reveal About Getting It Right When You Have To* (New York: Free Press, 2010)

7 Ibid.

Chapter Six

1 Joseph Loscalzo, "A Celebration of Failure," *Circulation* 129 (9), 2014: 953–55, doi:10.1161/CIRCULATIONAHA.114.009220.

2 Carol S. Dweck, *Mindset: The New Psychology of Success* (New York: Random House, 2006).

3 Elizabeth I. Martin, Kerry J. Ressler, Elisabeth Binder, and Charles B. Nemeroff, "The Neurobiology of Anxiety Disorders: Brain Imaging, Genetics, and Psychoneuroendocrinology," *Psychiatric Clinics of North America* 32 (3), 2009: 549–75, doi:10.1016/j.psc.2009.05.004.

4 Lang Chen, Se Ri Bae, Christian Battista, Shaozheng Qin, Tanwen Chen, et al., "Positive Attitude Toward Math Supports Early Academic Success: Behavioral Evidence and Neurocognitive Mechanisms," *Psychological Science* 29 (3), 2018: 390–402, doi:10.1177/0956797617735528.

5 William A. Cunningham and Philip David Zelazo, "Attitudes and Evaluations: A Social Cognitive Neuroscience Perspective," *Trends in Cognitive Science* 11 (3), 2007: 97–104, doi:10.1016/j.tics.2006.12.005.

6 Leo P. Crespi, "Quantitative Variation of Incentive and in the White Rat," *American Journal of Psychology* 55 (4), 1942: 467–517, doi:10.2307/1417120.

Chapter Seven

1 Sadia Najmi, Nader Amir, Kristen E. Frosio, and Catherine Ayers, "The Effects of Cognitive Load on Attention Control in Subclinical Anxiety and Generalised Anxiety Disorder," *Cognition and Emotion* 29 (7), 2015: 1210–23, doi:10.1080/02699931.2014.975188.

2 Steven E. Petersen and Michael I. Posner, "The Attention System

of the Human Brain: 20 Years After," *Annual Review of Neuroscience* 35 (2012): 73–89, doi:10.1146/annurev-neuro-062111-150525.

3 Adele Diamond, "Executive Functions," *Annual Review of Psychology* 64 (2013): 135–68, doi:10.1146/annurev-psych-113011-143750.

4 Morgan G. Ames, "Managing Mobile Multitasking: The Culture of iPhones on Stanford Campus," *CSCW '13: Proceedings of the 2013 Conference on Computer Supported Cooperative Work* (2013), 1487–98, doi:10.1145/2441776.2441945.

5 Antoine Lutz, Heleen A. Slagter, John D. Dunne, and Richard J. Davidson, "Attention Regulation and Monitoring in Meditation," *Trends in Cognitive Sciences* 12 (4), 2008: 163–69, doi:10.1016/j.tics.2008.01.005.

6 Matthieu Ricard, Antoine Lutz, and Richard J. Davidson, "Mind of the Meditator," *Scientific American* 311 (5), 2014: 39–45, doi:10.1038/scientificamerican1114-38; Lutz, Slagter, Dunne, and Davidson, "Attention Regulation and Monitoring in Meditation."

7 Heleen A, Slagter, Antoine Lutz, Lawrence L. Greischar, Andrew D. Francis, Sander Nieuwenhuis, et al., "Mental Training Affects Distribution of Limited Brain Resources," *PLoS Biology* 5 (6), 2007: doi:10.1371/journal.pbio.0050138.

8 Yi-Yuan Tang, Yinghua Ma, Junhong Wang, Yaxin Fan, Shigang Feng, et al., "Short-Term Meditation Training Improves Attention and Self-Regulation," *Proceedings of the National Academy of Sciences* 104 (43), 2007: 17152–56, doi:10.1073/pnas.0707678104.

9 Julia C. Basso and Wendy A. Suzuki, "The Effects of Acute Exercise on Mood, Cognition, Neurophysiology, and Neurochemical Pathways: A Review," *Brain Plasticity* 2 (2), 2017: 127–52, doi:10.3233/BPL-160040.

10 Stan J. Colcombe and Arthur F. Kramer, "Neurocognitive Aging and Cardiovascular Fitness: Recent Findings and Future Directions," *Journal of Molecular Neuroscience* 24 (2004): 9–14, doi:10.1385/JMN:24:1:009.

11 James A. Blumenthal, Michael A. Babyak, P. Muriali Doraiswamy, Lana Watkins, Benson M. Hoffman, Krista A. Barbour, Steve Herman, et al., "Exercise and Pharmacotherapy in the Treatment of Major Depressive Disorder," *Psychosomatic Medicine* 69 (7): 587–596, doi: 10.1097/PSY.0b013e318148c19a.

12 Gordon J. G. Asmundson, Mathew G. Fetzner, Lindsey B. Deboer, Mark B. Powers, Michael W. Otto, and Jasper A. J. Smits, "Let's Get Physical: A Contemporary Review of the Anxiolytic Effects of Exercise for Anxiety and Its Disorders," *Depression & Anxiety* 30 (4), 2013: 362–73, doi:10.1002/da.22043.

13 Stanley J. Colcombe, Kirk I. Erickson, Paige E. Scalf, Jenny S. Kim, Ruchika Prakash, et al., "Aerobic Exercise Training Increases Brain Volume in Aging Humans," *The Journals of Gerontology Series A* 61 (11), 2006: 1166–70, doi:10.1093/gerona/61.11.1166.

14 Basso and Suzuki, "The Effects of Acute Exercise on Mood, Cognition, Neurophysiology, and Neurochemical Pathways: A Review."

15 Joaquin A. Anguera, Jacqueline Boccanfuso, Jean L. Rintoul, Omar Al-Hashimi, Farshid Faraji, et al., "Video Game Training Enhances Cognitive Control in Older Adults," *Nature* 501 (7465), 2013: 97–101, doi:10.1038/nature12486; Federica Pallavicini, Ambra Ferrari, and Fabrizia Mantovani, "Video Games for Well-Being: A Systematic Review on the Application of Computer Games for Cognitive and Emotional Training in the Adult Population," *Frontiers in Psychology* 9 (2018): doi:10.3389/fpsyg.2018.02127.

Chapter Eight

1 Jack P. Shonkoff, "From Neurons to Neighborhoods: Old and New Challenges for Developmental and Behavioral Pediatrics," *Journal of Developmental & Behavioral Pediatrics* 24 (1), 2003: 70–76, doi:10.1097/00004703-200302000-00014.

2 Matthew D. Lieberman, "Social Cognitive Neuroscience: A Review of Core Processes," *Annual Review of Psychology* 58 (2007): 259–89, doi:10.1146/annurev.psych.58.110405.085654.

3 Heide Klumpp, Mike Angstadt, and K. Luan Phan, "Insula Reactivity and Connectivity to Anterior Cingulate Cortex When Processing Threat in Generalized Social Anxiety Disorder," *Biological Psychology* 89 (1), 2012: 273–76, doi:10.1016/j.biopsycho.2011.10.010.

4 Louise C. Hawkley and John T. Cacioppo, "Loneliness Matters: A Theoretical and Empirical Review of Consequences and Mechanisms," *Annals of Behavioral Medicine* 40 (2), 2010: 218–27, doi:10.1007/s12160-010-9210-8; Stephanie Cacioppo, John P. Capitanio, and John T. Cacioppo, "Toward a Neurology of Loneliness," *Psychological Bulletin* 140 (6), 2014: 1464–1504, doi:10.1037/a0037618.

5 Cigna, "New Cigna Study Reveals Loneliness at Epidemic Levels in America," May 1, 2018, https://www.cigna.com/about-us/newsroom/news-and-views/press-releases/2018/new-cigna-study-reveals-loneliness-at-epidemic-levels-in-america#:~:text=Research%20Puts%20Spotlight%20on%20the,U.S.%20and%20Potential%20Root%20Causes&text=The%20survey%20of%20more%20than,left%20out%20(47%20percent).

6 Julianne Holt-Lunstad, Timothy B. Smith, and J. Bradley Layton, "Social Relationships and Mortality Risk: A Meta-Analytic Review," *PLoS Medicine* 7 (7), 2010, doi:10.1371/journal.pmed.1000316.

7 Bhaskara Shelley, "Footprints of Phineas Gage: Historical Beginnings on the Origins of Brain and Behavior and the Birth of Cerebral Localizationism," *Archives of Medicine and Health Sciences* 4 (2), 2016: 280–86.

8 James M. Kilner and Roger N. Lemon, "What We Know Currently about Mirror Neurons," *Current Biology* 23, 2013: R1057-R1062. doi: 10.1016/j.cub.2013.10.051.

9 Frans B. M. de Waal and Stephanie D. Preston, "Mammalian Empathy: Behavioural Manifestations and Neural Basis," *Nature Reviews Neuroscience* 18 (8), 2017: 498–509, doi:10.1038/nrn.2017.72.

10 Giacomo Rizzolatti and Corrado Sinigalia, "The Mirror Mechanism: A Basic Principle of Brain Function," *Nature Reviews Neruoscience* 17 (12), 2016: 757–65, doi:10.1038/nrn.2016.135.

11 Claus Lamm, Jean Decety, and Tania Singer, "Meta-Analytic Evidence for Common and Distinct Neural Networks Associated with Directly Experienced Pain and Empathy for Pain," *Neuroimage* 54 (3), 2011: 2492–502, doi:10.1016/j.neuroimage.2010.10.014.

12 Claus Lamm and Jasminka Majdandzic, "The Role of Shared Neural Activations, Mirror Neurons, and Morality in Empathy—A Critical Comment," *Neuroscience Research* 90 (2015): 15–24, doi:10.1016/j.neures.2014.10.008.

13 Kevin A. Pelphrey and Elizabeth J. Carter, "Brain Mechanisms for Social Perception: Lessons from Autism and Typical Development," *Annals of the New York Academy of Sciences* 1145 (2008): 283–99, doi:10.1196/annals.1416.007.

14 Greg J. Norman, Louise C. Hawkley, Steve W. Cole, Gary G. Berntson, and John T. Cacioppo, "Social Neuroscience: The Social Brain, Oxytocin, and Health," *Social Neuroscience* 7 (1), 2012: 18–29, doi:10.1080/17470919.2011.568702; Candace Jones, Ingrid Barrera, Shaun Brothers, Robert Ring, and Claes Wahlestedt, "Oxytocin and Social Functioning," *Dialogues in Clinical Neuroscience* 19 (2), 2017: 193–201, doi:10.31887/DCNS.2017.19.2/cjones.

15 Thomas R. Insel, "The Challenge of Translation in Social Neuroscience: A Review of Oxytocin, Vasopressin, and Affiliative Behavior," *Neuron* 65 (6), 2010: 768–79, doi:10.1016/j.neuron.2010.03.005.

16 Norman, Hawkley, Cole, Berntson, and Cacioppo, et al., "Social Neuroscience: The Social Brain, Oxytocin, and Health."

17 Candace Jones, Ingrid Barrera, and Shaun Brothers, et al., "Oxytocin and Social Functioning," *Dialogues in Clinical Neuroscience* 19 (2), 2017: 193–201.

18 Daniel Goleman, *Working with Emotional Intelligence* (New York: Bantam Dell, 2006).

19 Daniel Goleman, *Social Intelligence: The New Science of Human Relationships* (New York: Bantam Books, 2006).

Chapter Nine

1 Arne Dietrich, "The Cognitive Neuroscience of Creativity," *Psychonomic Bulletin & Review* 11 (6), 2004: 1011–26, doi:10.3758/bf03196731.

2 Ibid.

3 Julie Burstein, *Spark: How Creativity Works* (New York: HarperCollins, 2011).

4 Arne Dietrich and Hilde Haider, "A Neurocognitive Framework for Human Creative Thought," *Frontiers in Psychology* 7 (2017), 2078: doi:10.3389/fpsyg.2016.02078.

5 Ibid.

6 M. Jung-Benjamin, E. M. Bowden, J. Haberman, J. L. Frymiare, S. Aranbel-Liu, et al., "Neural Activity When People Solve Verbal Problems with Insight," *PLoS Biology* 2 (4), April 2004: E97, doi:10.1371/journal.pbio.0020097.

7 Lindsey Carruthers, Rory MacLean, and Alexandra Willis, "The Relationship Between Creativity and Attention in Adults," *Creativity Research* 30 (4), 2018: 370–79, doi:10.1080/10400419.2018.1530910.

8 Randy L. Buckner, Jessica R. Andrews-Hanna, and Daniel L. Schacter, "The Brain's Default Network: Anatomy, Function, and Relevance to Disease," Annals of the New York Academy of Sciences 1124 (1), 2008: 1–38, doi.org/10.1196/annals.1440.011.

9 Roger E. Beaty, Yoed N. Kennett, Alexander P. Christensen, Monica D. Rosenberg, Mathias Benedek, Qunlin Chen, Andreas Fink et al., "Robust Prediction of Individual Creative Ability from Brain Functional Connectivity," *Proceedings of the National*

Academy of Sciences 115 (5), 2018: 1087–92, doi:10.1073/pnas.1713532115.

10 Peter, "The Cognitive Neuroscience of Creativity," *h+*, August 16, 2015, https://hplusmagazine.com/2015/07/22/the-cognitive-neuroscience-of-creativity/.

11 Scott B. Kaufman, 2007, "Creativity," in *Encyclopedia of Special Education*, 4th ed., Vol. 3, eds. Cecil R. Reynolds, Kimberly J. Vannest, and Elaine Fletcher-Janzen (New York: Wiley, 2014).

12 Lindsey Carruthers, Rory MacLean, and Alexandra Willis, "The Relationship Between Creativity and Attention in Adults," *Creativity Research* 30 (4), 2018: 370–79, doi:10.1080/10400419.2018.1530910.

13 Jiangzhou Sun, Qunlin Chen, Qinglin Zhang, Yadan Li, Haijiang Li, et al., "Training Your Brain to Be More Creative: Brain Functional and Structural Changes Induced by Divergent Thinking Training," *Human Brain Mapping* 37 (10), 2016: 3375–87, doi:10.1002/hbm.23246.

14 Julie Burstein, *Spark: How Creativity Works* (New York: HarperCollins, 2011).

PART THREE

1 James J. Gross and John P. Oliver, "Individual Differences in TwoEmotion Regulation Processes: Implications for Affect, Relationships, and Well-Being," *Journal of Personality and Social Psychology* 85 (2), 2003: 348–62, doi:10.1037/0022-3514.85.2.348.

2 Lisa Mosconi, *Brain Food: The Surprising Science of Eating for Cognitive Power* (New York: Aver, 2018).

3 Matthew Walker, *Why We Sleep* (New York: Scribner, 2017).

4 Lin-Manuel Miranda, *Gmorning, Gnight!: Little Pep Talks for Me & You* (New York: Random House, 2018).

5 Qing Li, "Effect of Forest Bathing Trips on Human Immune Function," *Environmental Health and Preventive Medicine* 15 (1), 2009:9–17, doi:10.1007%2Fs12199-008-0068-3.

6 Claire Eagleson, Sarra Hayes, Andrew Mathews, Gemma Perman, and Colette R. Hirsch, "The Power of Positive Thinking: Patho-

logical Worry Is Reduced by Thought Replacement in Generalized Anxiety Disorder," *Behaviour Research and Therapy* 78, 2016: 13–18, doi:10.1016/j.brat.2015.12.017.

7 Wendy Suzuki and Billie Fitzpatrick, *Healthy Brain, Happy Life: A Personal Program to Activate Your Brain & Do Everything Better* (New York: Dey Street, 2015).

INDEX

ABOUT THE AUTHORS

DR. WENDY SUZUKI is an award-winning professor of neural science and psychology at New York University and cofounder of BrainBody, an AI-based health tech company focused on mental health and wellness. As a neuroscientist, she is best known for her studies of the brain areas important for memory and her studies defining the effects of physical activity on the human brain and cognitive functions. She is an internationally bestselling author of the book *Healthy Brain, Happy Life*, which was made into a PBS special. Dr. Suzuki is a passionate thought leader and public speaker focusing on how physical activity can change and improve the brain, and now with this new book she offers innovative ways to approach everyday anxiety. Her TED Talk on the transformative effects of exercise on the brain was the second most popular TED Talk of 2018.

BILLIE FITZPATRICK is a writer, educator, and book collaborator who has coauthored numerous books in both fiction and nonfiction. She specializes in prescriptive titles related to wellness, sexuality, and relationships; neuroscience and brain-based behaviors; and motivational business.

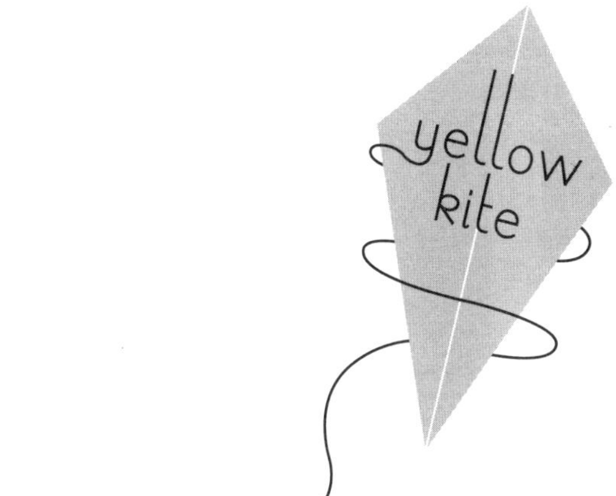

books to help you live a good life

Join the conversation and tell
us how you live a #goodlife